# the
# super easy
# teen
# cookbook

# the super easy **teen** cookbook

## 75 simple step-by-step recipes

### CHRISTINA HITCHCOCK

CALLISTO PUBLISHING

To Jim and Joey for
their unending love and
support. Everything I cook
for you, I make with love.

# Contents

Introduction
ix

**Chapter 1:** Getting in the Kitchen 1

**Chapter 2:** Breakfast and Smoothies 11

**Chapter 3:** Snacks, Sandwiches, and Appetizers 37

**Chapter 4:** Salads and Meat-Free Meals 71

**Chapter 5:** Meat and Seafood Meals 109

**Chapter 6:** Desserts 155

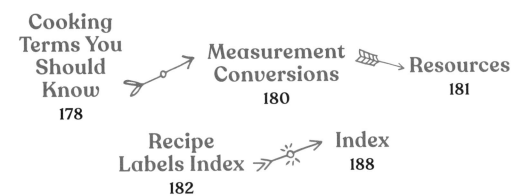

Cooking Terms You Should Know 178

Measurement Conversions 180

Resources 181

Recipe Labels Index 182

Index 188

# Introduction

**I have always loved being in the kitchen.** There is something about creating delicious food and sharing it with my family and friends that warms my soul. I grew up learning to cook from my mom and grandmothers. Later, I started watching cooking shows on PBS and the Food Network. I listened. I learned. I practiced what they taught me.

Learning how to cook at a young age taught me patience—especially when making bread—and it allowed me to explore my creative side. It also gave me confidence. There's nothing like making an amazing dish that everyone raves about to make you feel accomplished.

My goal for this cookbook is to help you develop your confidence in the kitchen. The recipes I've included were carefully written so you can make flavor-packed dishes that your family and friends will love.

I've also provided substitutions and adaptations for some recipes to allow you to explore your own creative side. Use my suggestions as inspiration, but don't feel confined by them. Experiment and try new ideas. And if it doesn't work out, that's okay. Failure is part of the process. Get back in there and try again.

Let's get into the kitchen and start making something delicious!

# Chapter 1
# Getting in the Kitchen

**If you're a teen who wants to learn how to cook, this cookbook is for you!** Cooking is fun and rewarding. You can learn to make your favorite restaurant dishes at home or experiment with new flavors and ingredients. Making food lets you use your creativity while nourishing yourself and, if you decide to share, nourishing others. This chapter will help you get organized so you can have a fun and successful cooking experience.

## BEFORE YOU START COOKING

**How these recipes work:** Each recipe in this book has easy-to-find ingredients and clear instructions. The recipes have lists to call attention to any particular tools and equipment you'll need, labels to flag the absence of common allergens, and more.

**Read the recipe twice:** Always read through the recipe two times before you start to cook. Make sure you have all of the ingredients and equipment necessary to make the recipe. When you're more confident in your skill set, you can (and should!) improvise in the kitchen more, but as you're getting the hang of how to cook, it's best to follow the recipe exactly as it's written.

**Make sure you have enough time:** Carefully review the recipe to ensure you have enough time to make it properly. Check the prep time, cook time, cooling time, marinating time, etc. You don't want to rush any of the steps.

**Take stock of your ingredients:** Before you shop for ingredients for a recipe, check to make sure you don't already have what you need. Be sure to check your pantry, fridge, and freezer before heading to the store.

**Set up your station:** Before you start cooking, make sure your workspace is clean, and pull together all of the equipment you need. You should also gather and prepare all the ingredients you'll be working with—chop the vegetables, grate the cheese, that sort of thing. Prepping ingredients before you start cooking makes the cooking process less stressful.

**Wash your produce:** Before you begin cooking, you should wash and dry all of your produce. Even produce that will be peeled needs to be washed because contaminants can transfer from your knife or peeler to the rest of your meal.

**Handle meat safely:** Keep raw meat in the refrigerator until shortly before you are ready to cook with it. Always wash your hands before and after handling raw meat, and be sure to use a dedicated knife and cutting board when preparing raw meat; in other words, don't use it for other non-meat ingredients. You definitely don't want to go through the trouble of safely cooking meat all the way through, only to chop up your parsley garnish on a cutting board that still has raw meat juices on it and then sprinkle parsley cross-contaminated with raw meat on your dinner!

**Wash your hands:** Always wash your hands with warm water and soap before you start cooking. Make sure you thoroughly clean the backs of your hands, your palms, and between your fingers.

**Clean as you go:** Take care of dirty dishes as you go along. Your workspace will be less cluttered, and you will have an easier time cleaning up the kitchen when you are finished cooking.

**Keep a garbage bowl on your workspace:** Designate a bowl specifically for trimmings and scraps. This is a quick and efficient way to manage waste while you're cooking.

**Measure properly:** When using measuring cups and spoons, heap the cup or spoon with the ingredient, then use a flat edge, such as a knife, to level it off. Use transparent measuring cups with varied measurements for liquid ingredients. Always measure liquid ingredients by placing the measuring cup on a flat surface and reading the measurement at eye level. If you're not looking straight at the little line, the view is distorted, and you could accidentally add the wrong amount of liquid to your recipe.

**Keep cooking:** Even if something doesn't turn out the way you expected, don't give up! Consider it a learning experience and try again. I know I just made a comment about how you should be careful to avoid accidentally adding the wrong amount of liquid to your recipe, but I also want to tell you that you shouldn't be too hard on yourself if not everything goes according to plan. Perfection is impossible, and it's not a realistic or healthy goal. We cannot dwell too much on imperfection because in life, mistakes are inevitable. Sometimes they even turn out to be unexpectedly delicious!

# Everything You'll Need

The following lists have the cookware, tools, and gadgets you will need to make the recipes in this book. Please be aware that you definitely don't need all of these items for every recipe; the most important tools to have are a chef's knife, a cutting board, and measuring tools.

## TOOLS AND UTENSILS

→ Chef's knife
→ Cutting board
→ Graters (1 rasp or fine grater, 1 box grater)
→ Ice cream scoop
→ Ladle
→ Measuring cups and spoons
→ Metal or plastic spatula
→ Pastry brush
→ Peeler
→ Rubber spatula
→ Serrated knife
→ Slotted spoon
→ Small, medium, and large bowls, for mixing
→ Stirring spoon
→ Strainer, preferably fine-mesh
→ Tongs
→ Whisk

## COOKWARE AND BAKEWARE

→ 9-by-9-inch baking dish, preferably metal
→ 12-cup cupcake pan
→ 13-by-18-inch rimmed baking sheet
→ 13-by-9-inch baking dish
→ Bundt pan
→ Large pot
→ Medium pot, preferably oven-safe
→ Pie plate
→ Small, medium, and large (4-quart) saucepans
→ Small, medium, and large (10- to 12-inch diameter) skillets, preferably nonstick
→ Wire rack

## OTHER

→ Blender
→ Can opener
→ Cupcake liners
→ Electric mixer (either a stand mixer or a handheld mixer)
→ Meat thermometer
→ Microwave
→ Parchment paper
→ Pot holder
→ Skewers
→ Toaster
→ Wax paper
→ Zip-top bags

# You Won't Believe What Your Microwave Can Do

Did you know that a microwave can do more than just reheat leftovers, make popcorn, and potentially start a dangerous fire if you put metal inside it and turn it on? In fact, the microwave is a versatile cooking appliance that is often underappreciated. You can use your microwave to make all sorts of things for breakfast, lunch, dinner, and even dessert—like these interesting (and quick and easy!) dishes:

**Sure, you've seen coffee in a mug, but have you seen egg in a mug?** Make a hearty breakfast in minutes. All you need is the aforementioned mug, an egg, and your favorite omelet toppings. Be sure to check out the recipe on page 16.

**Make crispy bacon without even turning on the stove.** Cooking bacon in a pan can be messy. But cooking crispy bacon in the microwave is a no-mess alternative.

**Chip away at your need for store-bought chips.** There's no need to deep-fry when you can make crispy potato chips in the microwave. The recipe is on page 49.

**Win brownie points by using the microwave to make the opposite of a brownie.** Yes, you can use your microwave to steam vegetables. Broccoli, green beans, baked potatoes, and corn on the cob—you name it, it's probably microwaveable.

**If you would like to make even more food items using a mug, may I suggest a small cake?** Satisfy your sweet tooth and whip up a warm single-serving cake in minutes using the microwave. Check out the Apple-Cinnamon Mug Cake on page 164.

# How to Avoid Getting Hurt

Kitchen safety is the most important part of cooking. There are a number of hazards in the kitchen that can cause you harm or serious injury. The most obvious one is probably knives, but I'm sure you'd be amazed to see what a box grater can do to a knuckle. That being said, cuts, burns, and sickness can be avoided by remembering a few important safety rules.

## DON'T CUT YOURSELF

→ Take your time when cutting. Focus on safety and precision, not speed.

→ Don't get distracted when using a knife. Focus on what you're cutting.

→ Keep your knives sharp. A dull knife is a dangerous knife that can lead to cuts and nicks. This is largely because you'll have to put more pressure on a dull knife when you're cutting. Therefore, if your finger is in the wrong spot at the wrong time, you could accidentally cut yourself more easily, with more force. Ask your guardians if they can keep the knives sharp or if they can teach you how to use a knife sharpener. Knives can also be taken to a professional sharpener.

→ Always cut on a stable surface, such as a cutting board. If the cutting board is moving around on your counter and doesn't seem to have a good grip, you can place a damp paper towel underneath it.

→ Always cut and peel away from yourself. You increase the risk of nicking or cutting yourself when you bring the blade toward you.

→ Never try to catch a falling knife. I'm sure you're an amazing person, but you aren't a cartoon action hero. Just let the knife fall so you don't risk grabbing the blade, then pick it up.

→ Don't place dirty knives in a sink with water. You don't want to reach into the water and accidentally cut yourself on an unseen blade. Instead, keep the dirty knife on the side and carefully clean it by hand.

## DON'T BURN YOURSELF

→ Always keep pot holders nearby when cooking. You especially want them within reach when you are working on the stove and transferring items to and from the oven.

→ Always keep pot handles turned inward so you don't accidentally knock the pot over. If the handle is jutting out over the edge of the stove where you and others walk, it's much easier to end up with a hot food spill.

→ Stand back when removing the lid from a hot pot or pan to avoid the steam buildup.

→ Don't wear clothing with loose-fitting sleeves when cooking. A loose sleeve is more likely to catch on fire.

→ When opening an oven, stand to the side so the steam doesn't hit you in the face.

→ When removing items from a hot oven, be careful you don't brush your arms or hands on the sides of the oven.

→ Make sure your pot holders are dry. If the pot holder is damp when you pick up something super hot, you could scald your hands.

→ Never walk away from items cooking on the stove. Pay attention to what you're cooking so it doesn't burn or catch fire.

→ In the event of a small grease fire on the stove, turn off the stove and smother the fire with a pot lid (not water) to cut off the air supply. If there's an oven fire, keep the oven door closed, turn off the oven, and call the fire department. Additionally, you should always keep a fire extinguisher in the kitchen.

→ Also note that, in addition to your sleeves, things like oven mitts, wooden utensils, food packaging, and kitchen towels can catch fire. Make sure you're not leaving flammable items on or near your stove.

## DON'T GET SICK

→ You should wash your hands frequently, and you must wash them after each time you handle raw meat. Use warm water and soap, making sure to thoroughly clean the backs of your hands, your palms, and between your fingers.

→ Check the expiration dates on your food to ensure everything is safe to eat.

→ Be careful of cross-contamination. Always use a different knife and cutting board when preparing raw meat. And again, wash your hands!

→ Cook your meats to the proper temperature. The only way to tell for sure if meat is fully cooked is to use a meat thermometer.

→ Refrigerate leftovers immediately after eating. Don't leave food sitting out at room temperature for long periods of time.

→ If you can't have gluten, always check ingredient packaging for gluten-free labeling (in order to ensure foods, especially oats, were processed in a completely gluten-free facility).

# 10 Items You Should Have in Your Pantry Right Now

Stocking your pantry with versatile essentials is the key to preparing delicious meals quickly and easily. Keeping a well-stocked pantry makes it easier to make meals without having to dash out to the store. As you run low on or run out of these items, add them to your grocery list immediately so you don't forget. Here, you'll find 10 items you should always have in your pantry. These basics are the building blocks of most recipes in this book.

1. **Starches:** Stock up on rice and a variety of dried pasta such as spaghetti, penne, and elbows. Rice and pasta can easily be transformed into hearty meals using jarred sauces or garlic and olive oil. You can even create meals using leftovers you have: Leftover rice can be used to make dishes like fried rice, rice pudding, and burrito bowls, and leftover pasta works in pasta salads, soups, and pasta bakes. Always make sure you cook pasta in salted water and don't rinse pasta after cooking.

2. **Stock:** Chicken and beef stock and vegetable broth add great flavor and are the base of many soups and sauces. I prefer using the low-sodium variety. Try cooking ramen noodles in flavored stock instead of using the seasoning packet. You can also cook rice in stock or broth rather than water for added flavor.

3. **Seasonings:** In addition to salt and pepper, spices and herbs add flavor and dimension to recipes. My go-tos are garlic powder, onion powder, dried thyme, and dried oregano.

4. **Garlic:** Fresh garlic is obviously delicious, and although it's a vegetable, it notably lasts for quite a while on the shelf (there's no need to refrigerate a bulb of fresh garlic). If you don't have fresh garlic, you can always substitute ½ teaspoon jarred minced garlic or ⅛ teaspoon garlic powder for 1 clove fresh garlic.

5. **Canola and olive oil:** Canola oil is a very versatile neutral oil, whereas olive oil is great to use when you want the oil to impart flavor to the dish.

6. **Soy sauce:** You can use soy sauce in complex sauces, marinades, dressings, and more to add a deeper flavor.

7. **Canned chicken and tuna:** Canned chicken and tuna are pantry staples. They can easily be turned into a quick meal or added to salads for protein.

8. **All-purpose flour:** All-purpose flour is a key ingredient in many baked goods. It also can be used as a thickener for sauces.

9. **Vanilla extract:** Vanilla extract is great for baking. It not only adds vanilla flavor to recipes but also helps enhance other flavors, such as chocolate. If you can, opt for pure vanilla extract over imitation vanilla.

10. **Nut butters:** Nut butters provide flavor, texture, and protein to recipes. They're great in sweet recipes, like smoothies and sundaes, and they can be used in savory dressings and sauces.

# Chapter 2
## Breakfast and Smoothies

Baked Vanilla French Toast 12

Fluffy Chocolate Chip Pancakes 14

Cheesy Microwave Scramble 16

The Perfect Omelet 19

Hard- and Soft-Boiled Eggs 21

Everything Bagel Avocado Toast 22

Apple-Cinnamon Baked Oatmeal 24

Snickerdoodle Overnight Oats 26

Cinnamon-Raisin Breakfast Couscous 28

Blueberry-Banana Smoothie Bowl 31

Matcha-Pineapple Smoothie 33

Strawberry Cheesecake Grilled Cheese 34

# Baked Vanilla French Toast

**Makes 8 pieces**
**Prep time: 5 minutes / Cook time: 20 minutes**
VEGETARIAN **NO SOY** NO NUTS

There's no need to stand over a hot griddle when you can make perfect French toast in the oven. This French toast requires little hands-on time and comes out golden and crisp on the outside and tender on the inside. Try it topped with powdered sugar and maple syrup, berries and whipped cream, chocolate syrup, or your own creative concoction.

**TOOLS AND EQUIPMENT**

*Rimmed baking sheet*

*Small saucepan*

*Large bowl*

*Measuring cups*

*Measuring spoons*

*Whisk*

*Metal spatula*

*Pot holder*

**INGREDIENTS**

Nonstick cooking spray, for coating the baking sheet

2 tablespoons unsalted butter

3 large eggs

1 tablespoon vanilla extract

2 teaspoons packed light brown sugar

1/2 teaspoon ground cinnamon

1/4 teaspoon table salt

1 cup milk

8 bread slices (brioche or challah are great options)

1. Place an oven rack in the lowest position and place another rack in the highest position. Preheat the oven to 425°F. Spray a rimmed baking sheet with nonstick cooking spray.

2. In a small saucepan, melt the butter over low heat. Make sure you're keeping a close eye on the butter and stirring it every minute or so, because butter can burn pretty quickly. Remove from the heat. Set aside to cool slightly.

3. Put the eggs, vanilla, brown sugar, cinnamon, and salt in a large bowl.

4. Whisk together the ingredients until they're fully combined. There should be no streaks of eggs left in the mixture.

5. Add the melted butter and the milk to the egg mixture. Whisk again until the mixture is completely combined.

6. Pour the egg mixture onto the prepared baking sheet, ensuring that it covers the entire baking sheet.

7. Place the bread slices in a single layer in the egg mixture.

8. Flip each piece of bread over, ensuring both sides are evenly coated in the egg mixture.

9. Place the baking sheet on the lower oven rack and bake for about 10 minutes.

10. Using a spatula, check the bottom of each slice. If the bottoms look golden brown, they're ready to move up in the oven. Do not flip the bread. Move the baking sheet to the top oven rack.

11. Switch the oven to broil. The broiler function radiates intense heat from the top of the oven, which is why you move the French toast up to the top rack.

12. Broil the French toast for 1 to 4 minutes, or until the top of the French toast is golden brown. Remove the baking sheet from the oven.

13. Flip the French toast over. Let sit on the rimmed baking sheet for 2 minutes so that it can steam slightly before serving.

14. Serve the French toast with maple syrup or any of your favorite toppings.

**TRY THIS!** Don't be afraid to get creative. Play around with the flavors of the egg mixture by swapping out the vanilla extract for almond extract, orange extract, or another flavor. You could also try swapping out regular bread for cinnamon-raisin bread.

Per serving (1 piece): Calories: 175; Total fat: 8g; Cholesterol: 79mg; Sodium: 238mg; Total carbohydrates: 19g; Fiber: 1g; Sugar: 7g; Protein: 6g

# Fluffy Chocolate Chip Pancakes

### Makes 8 pancakes
### Prep time: 10 minutes / Cook time: 50 minutes

VEGETARIAN  NO NUTS

This easy pancake recipe has been in my family for generations—I grew up eating these pancakes and now feed them to my family. It's easy to keep your pancakes warm while you're cooking. Simply place them on a rimmed baking sheet in a 250°F oven. If you have leftovers, you can easily store them in the fridge, then reheat them in a toaster or 250°F toaster oven.

**TOOLS AND EQUIPMENT**

*Large bowl*

*Stirring spoon*

*Measuring cups*

*Measuring spoons*

*Whisk*

*Large skillet*

*Plastic or metal spatula*

*Aluminum foil*

**INGREDIENTS**

1 cup all-purpose flour

2 tablespoons sugar

2 tablespoons baking powder

1/8 teaspoon table salt

1/8 teaspoon baking soda

1 cup milk

1/3 cup canola oil

1 large egg

2 teaspoons vanilla extract

Nonstick cooking spray, for coating the skillet

1/2 cup chocolate chips

1. In a large bowl, stir together the flour, sugar, baking powder, salt, and baking soda until fully combined. Be careful not to confuse the baking powder and the baking soda! They look alike, but baking soda has a weird flavor when you add too much of it.

2. To make the batter, add the milk, canola oil, egg, and vanilla to the flour mixture. Whisk together until thoroughly combined and there are no streaks of flour in the batter. Make sure you scrape down the sides and bottom of the bowl. The batter may be lumpy, but that's fine for pancakes.

3. Let the batter rest for 5 minutes while you prepare the skillet. This allows the flour to become hydrated by the liquid in the batter, giving you a lighter pancake texture.

4. Spray a large skillet with nonstick cooking spray and heat over medium-high heat.

5. Once the skillet is hot, using a ¼-cup measuring cup, pour ¼ cup of the pancake batter into the skillet. (Depending on the size of your skillet, you may be able to fit more than 1 pancake at a time.)

6. Sprinkle some chocolate chips on top of the pancake. You'll want to make sure you have enough chocolate chips for all 8 pancakes. Cook for 2 to 3 minutes, or until you see small air bubbles on the top of the pancake. Using a spatula, lift the side of the pancake and check the bottom. If it's golden brown, it's ready to flip.

7. Flip the pancake and cook for 2 to 3 more minutes, or until it's cooked through. If you find that the pancakes are browning before the centers are cooked through, turn the heat down a bit. Transfer to a plate and cover with aluminum foil.

8. Repeat with the remaining batter. Turn off the heat.

Per serving (1 pancake): Calories: 237; Total fat:14g; Cholesterol: 28mg; Sodium: 416mg; Total carbohydrates: 25g; Fiber: 1g; Sugar: 11g; Protein: 4g

## Switch It Up

**BLUEBERRY PANCAKES:** Make the pancake batter as described but replace the chocolate chips with 1 cup fresh or frozen blueberries (thawed if frozen). Add the blueberries to the pancake batter after it's been poured onto the skillet. Evenly distribute the blueberries among the pancakes.

**BANANA-WALNUT PANCAKES:** Make the pancake batter as described but replace the chocolate chips with chopped walnuts and 1 banana cut into ¼-inch-thick slices. Evenly distribute the walnuts and banana slices to the pancake batter after it's been poured onto the skillet.

**PINEAPPLE UPSIDE-DOWN PANCAKES:** Make the pancake batter as described. Drain a 20-ounce can of pineapple slices. After you pour ¼ cup of the pancake batter onto the skillet, add 1 pineapple slice to the center of the pancake. Add a maraschino cherry to the center of the pineapple ring. Sprinkle ½ teaspoon brown sugar on top of the pineapple.

# Cheesy Microwave Scramble

### Serves 1
### Prep time: 5 minutes / Cook time: 2 minutes

**VEGETARIAN** **NO GLUTEN** **NO SOY** **NO NUTS** **5 INGREDIENTS OR LESS** **REALLY FAST**

Ready in less than 10 minutes, this light and fluffy egg dish is perfect for busy mornings. Plus, you can easily customize it to fit your tastes with your favorite precooked veggies or breakfast meats. Serve it alongside a piece of avocado toast (page 22) for a heartier breakfast.

**TOOLS AND EQUIPMENT**

*Large microwave-safe mug*

*Measuring spoons*

*Fork*

*Grater*

*Microwave*

**INGREDIENTS**

Nonstick cooking spray, for coating the mug

2 large eggs

1 tablespoon milk

1 tablespoon grated Cheddar cheese

⅛ teaspoon table salt

Pinch ground black pepper

1. Spray the inside of a large microwave-safe mug with nonstick cooking spray. You'll want to make sure the mug is covered thoroughly so the egg doesn't stick.

2. Crack the eggs into the prepared mug and add the milk. Using a fork, mix until there are no more streaks of yolk or white, which is how you know it's well blended. Don't get too hung up on this, though—you're making a mug scramble, so it doesn't have to be perfect.

3. Add the cheese to the mug and season with the salt and pepper. Using a fork, stir until thoroughly combined. Microwave on high for 40 seconds.

4. Carefully remove the mug from the microwave—it may be hot—and stir the eggs with the fork.

5. Return the mug to the microwave and cook on high for 20 seconds.

6. Carefully remove the mug from the microwave and stir again.

7. Return the mug to the microwave and cook on high for 10 to 20 more seconds, or until the eggs have cooked through.

**DON'T HAVE IT?** No Cheddar cheese? No problem! You can use whatever cheese you have on hand. American, provolone, mozzarella, and Monterey Jack would all work great in this recipe. Just make sure you shred the cheese before adding it to the egg mixture. You can also use a soft cheese, such as goat cheese, and simply crumble it into the egg mixture.

Per serving: Calories: 190; Total fat: 13g; Cholesterol: 381mg; Sodium: 332mg; Total carbohydrates: 2g; Fiber: 0g; Sugar: 2g; Protein: 15g

# The Perfect Omelet

### Serves 1
### Prep time: 5 minutes / Cook time: 10 minutes
VEGETARIAN NO GLUTEN **NO SOY** NO NUTS **5 INGREDIENTS OR LESS FAST**

The key to mastering the omelet is to keep the eggs moving in the pan. You want to consistently move the liquid egg mixture to the edges of the omelet so it can cook properly. If you're planning to add any fillings (I provide some suggestions at the end of the recipe), make sure they are cooked or prepared before you start making the omelet.

**TOOLS AND EQUIPMENT**

*Large bowl*

*Whisk*

*10-inch nonstick skillet*

*Measuring spoons*

*Rubber spatula*

**INGREDIENTS**

2 large eggs

1 tablespoon unsalted butter

2 tablespoons milk

$\frac{1}{4}$ teaspoon table salt

Pinch ground black pepper

1. In a large bowl, whisk the eggs until they turn pale yellow in color.

2. Heat a 10-inch nonstick skillet over medium-low heat.

3. Once the skillet is hot, add the butter.

4. To the eggs, add the milk, salt, and pepper. Whisk again until the mixture is frothy.

5. Pour the egg mixture into the skillet. Do not stir the eggs. Let them sit for about 1 minute, or until the bottom of the egg mixture starts to set up and become semi-solid.

6. Starting on one side, using a rubber spatula, gently push the semi-set eggs toward the center of the skillet. Allow the liquid egg from the top to run onto the bare skillet (you may need to tilt the skillet slightly). Repeat this process, working your way around the skillet. When you're done, there should not be any liquid egg mixture on top of the omelet.

7. At this point, the omelet should easily move in the skillet. If it seems to be sticking, using a rubber spatula, loosen it around the edges.

*Continued on next page*

8. Using a rubber spatula, gently flip the omelet over. If you need assistance, try using a wider plastic spatula (generally speaking, you should not use a metal tool on a nonstick pan. If your skillet is ceramic coated, you definitely shouldn't use a metal tool, because metal scratches the ceramic). Briefly cook the omelet on the other side, for about 1 minute. You don't want it to get brown.

9. Using a rubber spatula, lift up one side of the omelet and fold it in half. Remove from the heat. Carefully transfer the omelet to a plate.

Per serving: Calories: 270; Total fat: 22g; Cholesterol: 405mg; Sodium: 818mg; Total carbohydrates: 3g; Fiber: 0g; Sugar: 3g; Protein: 14g

## Switch It Up

**VEGGIE OMELET:** Before starting the omelet, cut your veggies into bite-size pieces. Place 1 tablespoon butter in the skillet and cook the veggies for 4 to 5 minutes, or until they have softened. Transfer to a bowl. Prepare the omelet as described in the recipe, stopping at the step where you flip the omelet over. At this point, place ½ cup of the cooked vegetables on one half of the omelet. Fold the omelet as instructed in the recipe and serve. Bell peppers, onions, broccoli, mushrooms, and tomatoes are all great in this recipe.

**PIZZA OMELET:** Prepare the omelet as described in the recipe, stopping at the step where you flip the omelet over. At this point, place 2 tablespoons warmed marinara sauce (see the recipe on page 86) on one half of the omelet. Top with ¼ cup quartered pepperoni slices, ¼ cup shredded mozzarella cheese, and ½ teaspoon dried oregano. Fold the omelet as instructed in the recipe and serve.

# Hard- and Soft-Boiled Eggs

**Makes 6 eggs**

**Prep time: 5 minutes / Cook time: 10 to 15 minutes**

VEGETARIAN  NO DAIRY  NO GLUTEN  **NO SOY**  NO NUTS  **5 INGREDIENTS OR LESS**  FAST

Every cook should know how to make hard- and soft-boiled eggs. They are great in so many recipes, including salads, sandwiches, and noodle bowls. Using white vinegar in the water helps break down the shells as they boil, making the eggs easier to peel.

**TOOLS AND EQUIPMENT**

*Medium pot*

*Measuring spoons*

*Large bowl*

*Large slotted spoon*

**INGREDIENTS**

6 large eggs

1 teaspoon distilled white vinegar

Ice

1. Fill a medium pot with enough water to cover the eggs by 1 inch and bring the water to a boil over high heat. Add the vinegar.

2. Make an ice bath by filling a large bowl halfway with ice. Add water to fill the bowl within 2 inches of the top.

3. Once the water in the pot comes to a boil, reduce the heat to low to reduce the risk of burning yourself. Using a large spoon, carefully add the eggs to the pot one at a time, setting them down gently on the bottom.

4. Turn the heat back up and bring the water to a boil. Cook the eggs for 6 to 7 minutes for soft-boiled eggs and 12 to 14 minutes for hard-boiled eggs. Once the eggs have cooked to your desired doneness, turn off the heat, and using a large slotted spoon, carefully remove the eggs from the pot. Immediately—but gently—place the cooked eggs in the ice bath.

5. Let the eggs cool for 5 minutes before peeling.

**THERE'S SOME LEFT:** Store leftover unpeeled cooked eggs in the refrigerator. Hard-boiled eggs will last up to 1 week, and soft-boiled eggs will last for 2 days. To reheat soft-boiled eggs, using a large slotted spoon, place them in a single layer in a pot of simmering water. Simmering water will have tiny bubbles around the edge of the pot and 1 or 2 bubbles will break through the top of the surface every second or so. Simmer the eggs for about 45 seconds, then using a large spoon, remove them from the water.

Per serving (1 egg): Calories: 78; Total fat: 5g; Cholesterol: 187mg; Sodium: 62mg; Total carbohydrates: 1g; Fiber: 0g; Sugar: 1g; Protein: 6g

# Everything Bagel Avocado Toast

**Makes 2 slices**
**Prep time: 5 minutes**

**VEGAN  NO DAIRY  NO SOY  NO NUTS  5 INGREDIENTS OR LESS  REALLY FAST**

There are so many flavor combinations you can make with this simple avocado toast. Try the suggestions I provided or experiment with your own. This recipe calls for everything bagel seasoning, but you can also simply season with salt and pepper.

**TOOLS AND EQUIPMENT**

*Toaster*

*Chef's knife*

*Cutting board*

*Spoon*

*Small bowl*

*Measuring spoons*

*Fork*

**INGREDIENTS**

2 bread slices of choice

1 large ripe avocado

¼ teaspoon table salt

1 teaspoon everything bagel seasoning

1. Put the bread slices in the toaster and toast to desired doneness.
2. Using a chef's knife, cut the avocado lengthwise, maneuvering your knife around the pit. Firmly grip both sides of the avocado and twist around the pit to separate the halves. Using a spoon, scoop along the avocado skin to remove the flesh and put it in a small bowl. You can also just squish the avocado flesh out of the skin and into the bowl, if you want. Discard the avocado pit.
3. Add the salt to the avocado and using a fork, mash it to your desired consistency.
4. Spread half of the mashed avocado onto each slice of toast.
5. Sprinkle ½ teaspoon of everything bagel seasoning on top of each slice of toast.

Per serving (1 slice): Calories: 291; Total fat: 17g; Cholesterol: 0mg; Sodium: 642mg; Total carbohydrates: 31g; Fiber: 12g; Sugar: 6g; Protein: 7g

## Switch It Up

**SOFT-BOILED EGG AVOCADO TOAST:** Prepare the avocado toast as described, but instead of everything bagel seasoning, add a soft-boiled egg (page 21). Use a spoon to tap around the top of the egg to crack the shell. Remove the top portion of the shell, and using a spoon, scoop the egg out of the shell. Place the egg on top of the mashed avocado and sprinkle with salt and pepper to taste. Feel free to add a differently prepared egg, if you prefer!

**STREET CORN AVOCADO TOAST:** Prepare the avocado toast as described, but instead of everything bagel seasoning, add 2 tablespoons drained canned corn, 2 teaspoons crumbled Cotija cheese, ½ teaspoon chopped cilantro, a pinch of taco seasoning, and a squeeze of lime juice.

# Apple-Cinnamon Baked Oatmeal

### Serves 4
### Prep time: 15 minutes / Cook time: 40 minutes

**VEGETARIAN  NO GLUTEN  NO SOY  NO NUTS**

This recipe calls for apple and cinnamon, but you can easily swap out the apple for blueberries or strawberries. It's important that you use old-fashioned rolled oats in this, because quick-cooking or instant oats will absorb too much water and become mushy.

**TOOLS AND EQUIPMENT**

*13-by-9-inch baking dish*

*Measuring cups*

*Measuring spoons*

*Large bowl*

*Stirring spoon*

*Medium bowl*

*Whisk*

*Small microwave-safe bowl*

*Microwave*

*Peeler*

*Chef's knife*

*Cutting board*

*Pot holder*

**INGREDIENTS**

Nonstick cooking spray, for coating the baking dish

1½ cups old-fashioned gluten-free oats

¼ cup lightly packed light brown sugar

1 teaspoon ground cinnamon

¾ teaspoon baking powder

½ teaspoon table salt

⅛ teaspoon ground nutmeg

1¼ cups milk

1 large egg

½ teaspoon vanilla extract

2 tablespoons unsalted butter

1 large apple

1. Preheat the oven to 325°F. Spray the bottom and sides of a 13-by-9-inch baking dish with nonstick cooking spray.

2. Put the oats, brown sugar, cinnamon, baking powder, salt, and nutmeg in a large bowl. To measure the brown sugar, fill the measuring cup with the brown sugar and use your fingers or a spoon to lightly pack it into the measuring cup.

3. Stir the oat mixture to combine. The mixture will be crumbly and light brown in color.

4. Put the milk, egg, and vanilla in a medium bowl. Whisk until fully combined. The milk mixture will be light yellow with streaks of brown from the vanilla running through it.

5. Add the milk mixture to the oat mixture and stir until completely combined. The mixture will come together into a thick, wet batter.

6. Put the butter in a small microwave-safe bowl and microwave on high for 15 to 30 seconds, or until melted. Pour it into the batter and stir to combine.

7. Peel the apple, then remove the core: Place the apple upright on a cutting board and cut off 2 parallel sides, cutting as close to the core as possible. Cut off the remaining 2 sides, leaving a rectangular-shaped core. Discard the core. Chop the apple into ½-inch pieces. Spread them evenly over the bottom of the prepared baking dish.

8. Pour the batter on top of the apples.

9. Transfer the baking dish to the oven and bake for 35 to 40 minutes, or until the top is golden brown and the oatmeal is set and does not jiggle. Remove from the oven.

**THERE'S SOME LEFT:** If you have leftovers, you can reheat them in a 300°F oven for 5 to 10 minutes, or microwave on high for 30-second blasts to your desired temperature.

Per serving: Calories: 300; Total fat: 10g; Cholesterol: 66mg; Sodium: 485mg; Total carbohydrates: 46g; Fiber: 5g; Sugar: 24g; Protein: 8g

# Snickerdoodle Overnight Oats

**Serves 1**

**Prep time: 5 minutes, plus 8 hours to soak**

VEGAN  NO DAIRY  NO GLUTEN  **NO SOY**

**NO HEAT NECESSARY**

As you may have guessed from the name, you prepare overnight oats the night before you want them, and by morning, they're ready to eat. The key to getting the perfect consistency is a 2:1 liquid to oat ratio. You should use old-fashioned rolled oats and not instant oats, because oats made for speed will absorb too much water and become mushy.

**TOOLS AND EQUIPMENT**

*Container with tight-fitting lid*

*Measuring cups*

*Measuring spoons*

*Stirring spoon*

**INGREDIENTS**

½ cup gluten-free rolled oats

1 tablespoon light brown sugar

½ teaspoon chia seeds (optional)

½ teaspoon ground cinnamon

1 cup unsweetened almond milk

Extra brown sugar and cinnamon, for topping

1. Put the oats, brown sugar, chia seeds (if using), and cinnamon in a container with a tight-fitting lid. Stir to combine.
2. Top the container with the almond milk and stir to combine, pressing down on the oats to make sure they are completely submerged in the milk.
3. Cover the container with the lid and refrigerate overnight, or for at least 8 hours.
4. Sprinkle more brown sugar and cinnamon on top before eating.

Per serving: Calories: 268; Total fat: 6g; Cholesterol: 0mg; Sodium: 133mg; Total carbohydrates: 51g; Fiber: 5g; Sugar: 23g; Protein: 6g

## Switch It Up

**BLUEBERRY OVERNIGHT OATS:** Put ¼ cup fresh blueberries in the container. Top with the oat mixture and almond milk. Cover and refrigerate overnight. Sprinkle brown sugar and cinnamon on top before eating.

**STRAWBERRY-ALMOND OVERNIGHT OATS:** Chop ½ cup fresh strawberries after removing the stems. Put them in the container. Top with the oat mixture and almond milk. Sprinkle 2 tablespoons slivered almonds on top. Cover and refrigerate overnight. Sprinkle brown sugar and cinnamon on top before eating.

**PEANUT BUTTER OVERNIGHT OATS:** Put the almond milk, chia seeds, 2 tablespoons peanut butter, and 1 tablespoon maple syrup in the container. Stir to combine the ingredients, leaving swirls of peanut butter in the container. Top with the oats and stir again, making sure the oats are fully immersed in the milk. Cover and refrigerate overnight.

**CHOOSE YOUR OWN FROZEN FRUIT ADVENTURE:** You can use any type of frozen fruit in overnight oats, and there's no need to thaw the fruit beforehand. You can just put the frozen fruit in the bottom of the oats container, pour the oat mixture on top and stir in the almond milk. The frozen fruit will thaw in the fridge overnight.

# Cinnamon-Raisin Breakfast Couscous

**Serves 4**
**Prep time: 5 minutes / Cook time: 15 minutes**
VEGETARIAN **NO SOY** FAST

Couscous is sort of like a tiny pasta—it's a Maghrebi staple made of tiny little balls of crushed durum wheat. It's perfect for a quick and hearty breakfast. You can easily make this with your favorite nondairy milk substitute.

**TOOLS AND EQUIPMENT**

*Medium pot*

*Measuring cups*

*Stirring spoon*

*Measuring spoons*

.......................................

**INGREDIENTS**

1¼ cups milk

½ cup dried couscous

¼ cup raisins

¼ cup chopped walnuts

2 tablespoons light brown sugar

½ teaspoon ground cinnamon

⅛ teaspoon table salt

1. In a medium pot, heat the milk over low heat. Stir often until small bubbles appear around the edge of the pot.
2. Stir in the couscous, raisins, walnuts, brown sugar, cinnamon, and salt. Cover the pot with a lid and remove from the heat.
3. Let the couscous stand for 10 minutes. Resist the temptation to peek—couscous really is this easy, and it just needs time to steam and absorb the water. The mixture will thicken as it cools.

Per serving: Calories: 206; Total fat: 6g; Cholesterol: 4mg; Sodium: 78mg; Total carbohydrates: 33g; Fiber: 2g; Sugar: 15g; Protein: 7g

## Switch It Up

**BANANA-WALNUT BREAKFAST COUSCOUS:** Prepare the recipe as described, without the raisins. When you remove the couscous pot from the burner, stir in ½ cup chopped walnuts. Before you serve the couscous, top each bowl with sliced bananas.

**STRAWBERRY-PECAN BREAKFAST COUSCOUS:** Prepare the recipe as described, without the raisins. When you remove the couscous pot from the burner, stir in ½ cup chopped pecans. Before you serve the couscous, top each bowl with sliced strawberries.

**BLUEBERRY BREAKFAST COUSCOUS:** Prepare the recipe as described, without the raisins. When you remove the couscous pot from the burner, stir in ½ cup sliced almonds. Before you serve the couscous, top each bowl with ¼ cup fresh blueberries.

# Blueberry-Banana Smoothie Bowl

## Serves 1
## Prep time: 5 minutes

VEGETARIAN  NO GLUTEN  **NO SOY**  NO HEAT NECESSARY  REALLY FAST

Smoothie bowls are not only photogenic but also delicious. You can customize the flavors to suit your tastes and get creative with the toppings. Plus, you can really pack in the nutrients by adding spinach, kale, or açai. Try adding some Maple Granola with Cranberries (page 51) for crunch.

**TOOLS AND EQUIPMENT**

*Blender*

*Measuring cups*

*Measuring spoons*

*Rubber spatula*

*Chef's knife*

*Cutting board*

**INGREDIENTS**

1/3 cup frozen banana pieces or 1/2 frozen banana

3/4 cup unsweetened almond milk

3/4 cup fresh or frozen blueberries

1/2 cup fresh or frozen raspberries

1/4 cup plain Greek yogurt

1 tablespoon chia seeds (optional)

........................................

**SUGGESTED TOPPINGS**

1/2 fresh banana, cut into 1/4-inch-thick slices

1/4 cup fresh blueberries

1/4 cup fresh raspberries

1 teaspoon chia seeds

1 tablespoon honey

1. In a blender, combine the banana, almond milk, blueberries, raspberries, yogurt, and chia seeds (if using). Blend until smooth. Using a rubber spatula, scrape down the sides of the blender to ensure everything is blended.

2. Pour the smoothie into a bowl.

Continued on next page

3. Add the toppings to the smoothie as desired. You can just pile them on top, or you can arrange the toppings in beautiful rows, depending on your mood.

Per serving: Calories: 267; Total fat: 7g; Cholesterol: 12mg; Sodium: 140mg; Total carbohydrates: 51g; Fiber: 9g; Sugar: 35g; Protein: 6g

## Switch It Up

**CHOCOLATE, PEANUT BUTTER, AND BANANA SMOOTHIE BOWL:** Prepare the recipe as described, substituting equal amounts of peanut butter and chocolate syrup for the blueberries and raspberries in the smoothie—1 tablespoon of each works great, but you can adjust the amounts to suit your taste. Top the smoothie bowl with banana slices, Maple Granola with Cranberries (page 51), and chopped peanuts.

**TROPICAL SMOOTHIE BOWL:** Prepare the smoothie recipe as described, substituting equal amounts of fresh or canned pineapple chunks and fresh or frozen mango chunks for the blueberries and raspberries. Top the smoothie bowl with ½ fresh banana, sliced; ¼ cup canned mandarin orange segments; ¼ cup coconut flakes; 1 teaspoon chia seeds; and 1 tablespoon honey.

# Matcha-Pineapple Smoothie

### Serves 1
### Prep time: 5 minutes

VEGETARIAN  NO GLUTEN  **NO SOY**  NO NUTS  **NO HEAT NECESSARY**
**5 INGREDIENTS OR LESS**  REALLY FAST

Matcha, a green tea powder popular in Japan and China, is packed with antioxidants. If you find that the matcha powder gives the smoothie a bitter taste, you can add three or four more frozen pineapple chunks and blend again until smooth. And though spinach may seem like an odd choice for a smoothie, it's full of vitamins, and you won't even taste it.

**TOOLS AND EQUIPMENT**

*Blender*

*Measuring cups*

*Measuring spoons*

*Rubber spatula*

......................................

**INGREDIENTS**

½ cup packed baby spinach

1 cup frozen pineapple chunks

½ cup vanilla Greek yogurt

1 tablespoon ground flaxseed (optional)

½ teaspoon matcha green tea powder

Milk, nondairy milk, or water, as needed

1. In a blender, combine the spinach, pineapple, yogurt, flaxseed (if using), and matcha powder. Blend until smooth. Using a rubber spatula, scrape down the sides of the blender to ensure everything is blended.

2. If the smoothie is too thick, add milk, 1 tablespoon at a time, blending after each tablespoon, until the smoothie has reached your desired consistency.

**DON'T HAVE IT?** The frozen pineapple chunks give the smoothie its icy texture. If you don't have frozen pineapple chunks, you can use ½ cup fresh or canned pineapple chunks and 3 or 4 ice cubes.

Per serving: Calories: 215; Total fat: 4g; Cholesterol: 13mg; Sodium: 53mg; Total carbohydrates: 31g; Fiber: 2g; Sugar: 24g; Protein: 12g

# Strawberry Cheesecake Grilled Cheese

### Serves 1
### Prep time: 5 minutes / Cook time: 10 minutes
VEGETARIAN **NO SOY** NO NUTS **5 INGREDIENTS OR LESS FAST**

Grilled cheese for breakfast? Absolutely! This creamy and sweet sandwich is the perfect combination of flavors and textures. I like to use brioche bread sliced thick, because it's rich and soft and toasts up perfectly.

**TOOLS AND EQUIPMENT**

*Measuring spoons*

*Chef's knife*

*Cutting board*

*Skillet*

*Plastic or metal spatula*

..................................

**INGREDIENTS**

3 tablespoons strawberry cream cheese spread or regular cream cheese, at room temperature

2 bread slices of choice

1 tablespoon strawberry jam

2 large strawberries

3 tablespoons unsalted butter, at room temperature, divided

1. Spread the cream cheese evenly onto the bread slices.
2. Add the jam to 1 bread slice, on top of the cream cheese layer.
3. Remove the stems from the strawberries and cut the strawberries into thin slices.
4. Place in a single layer on top of the jam.
5. Assemble the sandwich, placing the other slice of bread on top of the cream cheese and strawberry bread.
6. Generously butter the outside (on both sides of the sandwich) using 1 tablespoon of butter per side.
7. In a skillet, melt the remaining 1 tablespoon of butter over medium-high heat.
8. Put the sandwich in the skillet and toast for 2 to 3 minutes, or until lightly browned.
9. Using a plastic or metal spatula, flip the sandwich and cook for 2 to 3 more minutes, or until the other side is lightly browned. Remove from the heat.

Per serving: Calories: 742; Total fat: 49g; Cholesterol: 129mg; Sodium: 754mg; Total carbohydrates: 67g; Fiber: 11g; Sugar: 30g; Protein: 12g

# Chapter 3
# Snacks, Sandwiches, and Appetizers

Classic Guacamole 38

Loaded Sheet Pan Nachos 40

Bacon and Cheese Tater Tot Kebabs 42

Crispy Mozzarella Cheese Sticks 44

Oven-Toasted Ravioli 46

Sweet and Salty Trail Mix 48

Microwave Potato Chips 49

Maple Granola with Cranberries 51

Taco Tartlets 54

Buffalo Cauliflower Bites 56

Peanut Butter and Banana Panini 58

Classic Turkey Club Sandwiches 61

Roasted Chicken Salad Pitas 63

Steak and Cheese Hand Pies 65

Ham and Cheese Pinwheels 68

# Classic Guacamole

**Serves 4**
**Prep time: 10 minutes**

**VEGAN  NO DAIRY  NO GLUTEN  NO SOY  NO NUTS  NO HEAT NECESSARY  REALLY FAST**

Avocados have been cultivated for thousands of years in the region we now call Mexico, and guacamole is the quintessential way to enjoy avocado, which is technically a large berry!

**TOOLS AND EQUIPMENT**

*Chef's knife*

*Cutting board*

*Medium bowl*

*Fork*

*Measuring spoons*

*Small spoon*

*Measuring cups*

**INGREDIENTS**

3 ripe avocados

1 lime

1 teaspoon table salt

2 Roma tomatoes

1 red onion

1 garlic clove

1 jalapeño

3 tablespoons chopped fresh cilantro

1. Using a chef's knife, cut 1 avocado lengthwise, maneuvering your knife around the pit. Firmly grip both sides of the avocado and twist around the pit to separate the halves. Squeeze the avocado flesh into a medium bowl. Discard the avocado pit, or save it to put in the dip if you think you'll have leftover guacamole and you want to use the pit to slow down the browning process.

2. Repeat with the remaining avocados.

3. On a solid surface, press down firmly on the lime as you roll it around—this helps break up the cells in citrus and makes it easier to juice later. You don't need to really squish the lime, but don't be shy with the pressure. Cut the lime in half and squeeze the juice into the bowl. If you are having trouble squeezing the juice from the lime, using a fork, stab the lime flesh, and turn it a quarter turn to help release the juice.

4. Add the salt to the bowl and using a fork, mash the avocado mixture until you have your desired consistency.

5. Cut each tomato in half and remove the seeds (or most of the seeds—this doesn't have to be perfect). Using a spoon, crush the tomatoes a little and cut them into ¼-inch pieces. Add to the bowl.

6. Cut the onion into ¼-inch dice: Start by cutting the onion in half from root to tip. Peel off the papery outside layer and a layer of onion underneath that. For each onion half, cut off the tip of the onion, but leave the root end intact. Cut each onion half in half again from root to tip. Place an onion quarter, flat-side down, on a cutting board. Make several vertical cuts from end to end, being careful not to cut through the root end. Flip the onion quarter onto the other flat side and repeat the vertical cuts, again being careful not to cut through the root end. Then cut the onion crosswise into even ¼-inch dice—the pieces should just fall off the knife ready to go. You can make the dice as thick or as thin as you need. Add ½ cup to the bowl and store any leftover onion.

7. Press the garlic clove so it gets a little squished, then peel off the papery layer and cut off the root end (the nubby side). Mince the garlic: Moving the knife blade in a rocking motion, run the knife over the squished clove repeatedly. Use the knife blade to turn the pile of cut garlic a quarter turn every few seconds. Continue this until the garlic is cut into very fine pieces (minced), then add to the bowl.

8. Cut the top ⅛ inch off the jalapeño. Cut the jalapeño lengthwise in half. Using a spoon, scrape out the seeds and white rib, or leave the seeds for a spicier guacamole. Cut the jalapeño into a very fine dice. Be sure to wash your hands afterward and be careful to not touch your face.

9. Add the cilantro and jalapeño to the bowl and stir to combine.

10. If you have to refrigerate this before serving, place a layer of plastic wrap on top, gently pressing it directly on top of the mixture.

OOPS . . . Can't find ripe avocados? No problem! You can easily speed the process up at home. Preheat the oven to 200°F. Wrap each avocado in aluminum foil and put it on a rimmed baking sheet. Put the baking sheet in the oven and bake for 10 minutes, or until the avocados have softened. Depending on how hard the avocado is, it could take longer than 10 minutes; if you need to leave them in the oven longer, keep checking the avocados every minute or so. Once softened, remove the avocados from the oven and refrigerate them until cooled. Remove the foil and use as directed.

Per serving: Calories: 192; Total fat: 16g; Cholesterol: 0mg; Sodium: 601mg; Total carbohydrates: 14g; Fiber: 8g; Sugar: 3g; Protein: 3g

# Loaded Sheet Pan Nachos

**Serves 2**
**Prep time: 5 minutes / Cook time: 15 minutes**
NO GLUTEN **NO SOY** NO NUTS FAST

If you don't have time to cook ground beef for these nachos, use cooked chicken from a store-bought rotisserie chicken. Simply remove the chicken from the bone and shred it with your hands or chop into bite-size pieces. For topping ideas, try sliced avocado, chopped fresh cilantro leaves, sliced black olives, and sour cream.

**TOOLS AND EQUIPMENT**

*Rimmed baking sheet*

*Large skillet*

*Measuring spoons*

*Stirring spoon*

*Measuring cups*

*Small heat-safe bowl*

*Can opener*

*Strainer*

*Chef's knife*

*Cutting board*

*Pot holder*

.................................

**INGREDIENTS**
Nonstick cooking spray, for coating the baking sheet

2 teaspoons canola oil

½ pound ground beef

½ teaspoon garlic powder

½ teaspoon onion powder

¼ teaspoon table salt

Pinch ground black pepper

½ cup canned black beans

¼ cup canned corn

1 (4-ounce or individual-size) bag corn tortilla chips

½ cup shredded Monterey Jack cheese

1 Roma tomato

1 red onion

½ jalapeño

1. Preheat the oven to 400°F. Spray a rimmed baking sheet with nonstick cooking spray.

2. In a large skillet, heat the canola oil over medium-high heat until it shimmers.

3. Add the beef. Using a spoon, break up the beef.

4. Sprinkle the garlic powder, onion powder, salt, and pepper over the raw beef.

5. Continue breaking up the beef as it cooks so that it resembles crumbles. Cook for about 5 minutes, or until no longer pink. Remove from the heat.

6. In order to properly discard the excess fat, you need to drain it off. Push the beef to one side of the pan and slowly tilt the pan, allowing the fat to pool on the other side. Then using a spoon, transfer the fat into a heat-safe bowl. Be sure to use a buffer for your hands or any surfaces when you're moving the bowl of fat—it will be very hot. Set the fat aside to cool; later, when it's cool, scoop it into the trash. You don't want to flush fats and oils down the sink because they will clog pipes.

7. Drain the black beans and corn in a strainer, then rinse with cold water.

8. Lay the tortilla chips on the prepared baking sheet in an even layer. Top with the cooked beef, black beans, and corn. Sprinkle an even layer of the shredded cheese on top.

9. Transfer the baking sheet to the oven and bake for 5 to 6 minutes, or until the cheese melts. Remove from the oven.

10. Meanwhile, cut the tomato into 1/4-inch pieces.

11. Cut the onion into 1/4-inch dice: Start by cutting the onion in half from root to tip. Peel off the papery outside layer and a layer of onion underneath that. For each onion half, cut off the tip of the onion, but leave the root end intact. Cut an onion half in half again from root to tip. Place an onion quarter, flat-side down, on a cutting board. Make several vertical cuts from end to end, being careful not to cut through the root end. Flip the onion quarter onto the other flat side and repeat the vertical cuts, again being careful not to cut through the root end. Then cut the onion crosswise into even 1/4-inch dice—the pieces should just fall off the knife ready to go. Set 2 tablespoons aside and store any leftover onion.

12. Cut the top 1/8 inch off the jalapeño. Cut the jalapeño lengthwise in half. Using a spoon, scrape out the seeds and white rib, or leave the seeds for spicier nachos. Cut the jalapeño into a very fine dice. Be sure to wash your hands afterward and be careful to not touch your face.

13. Top the nachos with the tomato, onion, and jalapeño. Add the toppings as desired.

TRY THIS! Make these nachos meatless by substituting 8 ounces vegetarian canned refried beans for the ground beef mixture. Heat up the beans on the stove in a small saucepan, whisking in water and then heating over medium heat until they reach your desired consistency.

Per serving: Calories: 774; Total fat: 42g; Cholesterol: 125mg; Sodium: 933mg; Total carbohydrates: 56g; Fiber: 9g; Sugar: 3g; Protein: 45g

# Bacon and Cheese Tater Tot Kebabs

**Makes 4 kebabs**
**Prep time: 10 minutes / Cook time: 30 minutes**
NO GLUTEN **NO SOY** NO NUTS

There is nothing more fun than food on a stick! You can use traditional tater tots for this recipe or swap them out for sweet potato tots or veggie tots. These kebabs are great served alongside the Cowboy Burgers on (page 112). For added flavor, you can dip the tots in barbecue sauce or ranch dressing.

**TOOLS AND EQUIPMENT**

*Wooden or metal skewers*

*13-by-9-inch baking dish*

*2 rimmed baking sheets*

*Pot holder*

*Parchment paper*

*Grater*

*Measuring cups*

*Measuring spoons*

*Small bowl*

*Stirring spoon*

*Chef's knife*

*Cutting board*

.......................................

**INGREDIENTS**

24 frozen tater tots

¼ cup grated Monterey Jack cheese

⅛ teaspoon garlic powder

⅛ teaspoon onion powder

¼ cup packaged real bacon bits

1 scallion

1. Preheat the oven to 425°F. If you're using wooden skewers, place them in a 13-by-9-inch baking dish filled with water to soak for at least 20 minutes, if not longer. This will prevent them from burning in the oven.

2. Put the tater tots on a rimmed baking sheet and bake according to the package directions, usually 20 to 25 minutes. Remove from the oven.

3. Let the tater tots cool for 5 minutes.

4. While the tater tots are baking, line another rimmed baking sheet with parchment paper or spray with nonstick cooking spray. If you're using wooden skewers, remove them from the water, and using paper towels, pat dry.

5. Place 6 tater tots on each skewer and place them on the prepared baking sheet.

6. Put the cheese, garlic powder, and onion powder in a small bowl. Stir to combine. You should be aiming for an even coating of spices.

7. Sprinkle the cheese mixture over the skewers, making sure each skewer is evenly coated, followed by the bacon bits.

8. Trim the scallion by cutting off the root end and cutting ½ inch off the top. Cut the remaining scallion crosswise, so you have little circles of scallion. Evenly distribute among the skewers.

9. Return the tater tots to the oven and bake for 5 minutes, or until the cheese has melted. Remove from the oven.

**DON'T HAVE IT?** If you don't have skewers, you can easily make this recipe by placing the baked tater tots on a rimmed baking sheet, making sure the tots are close together before adding the cheese, bacon, and scallion. Then, you can eat them like nachos (or . . . like tater tots).

Per serving (1 kebab): Calories: 159; Total fat: 8g; Cholesterol: 13mg; Sodium: 497mg; Total carbohydrates: 14g; Fiber: 1g; Sugar: 1g; Protein: 5g

# Crispy Mozzarella Cheese Sticks

### Serves 2
### Prep time: 20 minutes, plus 30 minutes to freeze / Cook time: 15 minutes
**VEGETARIAN NO SOY NO NUTS**

In this recipe, the mozzarella sticks are baked in the oven instead of deep-fried. You can assemble the cheese sticks through step 9 and leave them in the freezer to eat later. When you're ready to eat them, simply bake the frozen cheese sticks according to the recipe instructions.

**TOOLS AND EQUIPMENT**

*Rimmed baking sheet*

*Aluminum foil*

*Chef's knife*

*Cutting board*

*Measuring cups*

*Measuring spoons*

*3 shallow bowls (1 microwave-safe)*

*Fork*

*Microwave*

*Stirring spoon*

*Tongs*

*Pot holder*

......................................

**INGREDIENTS**

Nonstick cooking spray, for coating the baking sheet

3 mozzarella cheese sticks (string cheese)

2 tablespoons all-purpose flour

1 large egg

1 tablespoon water

1 tablespoon unsalted butter

½ cup seasoned bread crumbs

½ cup panko bread crumbs

1 teaspoon table salt

⅛ teaspoon ground black pepper

½ cup marinara sauce

1. Line a rimmed baking sheet with aluminum foil and spray with nonstick cooking spray.

2. Cut each cheese stick in half. Each piece of cheese should be about 3 inches long, which is the ideal size for an appetizer portion.

3. Put the flour in a shallow bowl.

4. Put the egg and water in another shallow bowl and using a fork, beat until combined.

5. Put the butter in a microwave-safe shallow bowl and microwave on high for 15 seconds, or until the butter has melted. You can also melt the butter in a small saucepan on the stove.

6. To the melted butter, add the seasoned bread crumbs, panko bread crumbs, salt, and pepper. Stir to combine.

7. Each piece of cheese will be dredged in a 5-layer coating: 1) Roll the cheese in the flour until it is evenly coated. 2) Roll the cheese in the egg mixture until it's completely coated. 3) Roll the cheese in the bread crumb mixture. 4) Roll the cheese in the egg mixture again. 5) Roll the cheese in the bread crumb mixture, pressing the crumbs so they completely coat the cheese. To recap, you're going to do a flour roll, an egg roll, a bread crumb roll, an egg roll, then one last bread crumb roll.

8. When they're coated, place the cheese sticks in a single layer on the prepared baking sheet.

9. Cover the baking sheet with plastic wrap or foil and freeze for 30 minutes. This will help the cheese and breading hold together better when the sticks are in the oven.

10. When ready to bake, place an oven rack in the middle position and preheat the oven to 415°F.

11. Transfer the baking sheet to the oven and bake for 15 minutes, flipping the cheese sticks using tongs halfway through baking. Remove from the oven.

12. Let the cheese sticks cool for at least 5 minutes to avoid a scalding cheese burn on the roof of your mouth, then serve with the marinara sauce on the side.

**THERE'S SOME LEFT:** If you have cheese sticks left over, you can store them in the fridge and easily reheat them by baking them in a 300°F oven for 5 to 10 minutes.

Per serving: Calories: 475; Total fat: 20g; Cholesterol: 120mg; Sodium: 2203mg; Total carbohydrates: 50g; Fiber: 3g; Sugar: 8g; Protein: 21g

# Oven-Toasted Ravioli

**Serves 4**
**Prep time: 15 minutes / Cook time: 15 minutes**
VEGETARIAN **NO SOY** NO NUTS

These toasted ravioli are a great appetizer or snack. They are crispy on the outside but soft and tender on the inside. If you use frozen ravioli, you must thaw them before preparing the recipe—the bread crumb coating will not stick if they are frozen. Serve these toasted ravioli with the homemade marinara sauce on page 86 for dipping.

**TOOLS AND EQUIPMENT**

*Wire rack*

*Rimmed baking sheet*

*Measuring cups*

*Measuring spoons*

*2 shallow bowls*

*Fork*

*Stirring spoon*

*Pot holder*

..................................

**INGREDIENTS**

Nonstick cooking spray, for coating

2 large eggs

2 tablespoons water

1 cup panko bread crumbs

¼ cup grated vegetarian parmesan cheese

2 teaspoons Italian seasoning

1 teaspoon garlic powder

1 teaspoon table salt

1 pound fresh or frozen cheese ravioli (thawed if frozen)

Marinara sauce, for dipping

1. Place an oven rack in the lower-middle position and preheat the oven to 425°F. Place a wire rack on top of a rimmed baking sheet and spray the rack with nonstick cooking spray. The wire rack will allow the hot air to circulate around the ravioli and cook it evenly on the top and bottom. If you don't have a wire rack, you can use the wire rack from a toaster oven.

2. Put the eggs and water in a shallow bowl and, using a fork, beat until combined. The eggs should be pretty much streak-free.

3. Put the panko bread crumbs, parmesan cheese, Italian seasoning, garlic powder, and salt in another shallow bowl. Stir to combine so that everything is evenly distributed.

4. Dunk 1 ravioli in the egg mixture, coating the entire outside.

5. Next, dunk it in the bread crumb mixture to coat the outside. Gently press the crumbs into the ravioli to ensure the coating sticks.

6. Repeat with the remaining ravioli, placing each coated ravioli on the prepared baking sheet when the dunking and coating is finished. Be sure to leave at least 1 inch between the ravioli so they don't get stuck together in the oven.

7. When all the ravioli are coated and on the rack, spray the tops with a little nonstick cooking spray.

8. Transfer the baking sheet to the oven and bake for 15 minutes, or until the tops are crispy and golden brown. Remove from the oven.

9. Serve the ravioli with marinara sauce on the side.

OOPS . . . If the ravioli are getting too brown before they are cooked through, cover them lightly with some aluminum foil.

Per serving: Calories: 331; Total fat: 11g; Cholesterol: 199mg; Sodium: 1504mg; Total carbohydrates: 42g; Fiber: 2g; Sugar: 2g; Protein: 15g

# Sweet and Salty Trail Mix

**Makes about 2½ cups**
**Prep time: 5 minutes**
VEGETARIAN  NO HEAT NECESSARY  REALLY FAST

This snack mix is a satisfying combination of sweet, salty, crunchy, and chewy. You can easily double or triple the recipe so you always have some on hand for a snack. This is an almost endlessly customizable recipe, so be sure to check out the tips for substitutions.

**TOOLS AND EQUIPMENT**
*Measuring cups*
*Large bowl*
*Stirring spoon*
*Airtight container*

......................................

**INGREDIENTS**
½ cup pecans
½ cup almonds
½ cup dried banana chips
⅓ cup dried cranberries
½ cup oyster crackers
¼ cup semisweet chocolate chips

Put the pecans, almonds, banana chips, dried cranberries, crackers, and chocolate chips in a large bowl. Stir until completely combined. Store in an airtight container.

Per serving (½ cup): Calories: 287; Total fat: 19g; Cholesterol: 0mg; Sodium: 50mg; Total carbohydrates: 29g; Fiber: 4g; Sugar: 19g; Protein: 5g

## Switch It Up

**CHOCOLATE AND PRETZEL TRAIL MIX:** Prepare the recipe as described, but swap out the cranberries for white chocolate chips and swap out the oyster crackers for mini pretzel twists.

**TROPICAL TRAIL MIX:** Prepare the recipe as described, but swap out the pecans for cashews, swap out the cranberries for dried pineapple pieces, and swap out the semisweet chocolate chips for yogurt-covered raisins.

# Microwave Potato Chips

**Serves 2**

**Prep time: 10 minutes / Cook time: 10 minutes**

VEGAN  NO DAIRY  NO GLUTEN  **NO SOY**  NO NUTS

**5 INGREDIENTS OR LESS  FAST**

These potato chips are so light and crispy that it's hard to believe they're made in the microwave. They're the perfect side for Classic Turkey Club Sandwiches (page 61). A fun fact about potatoes: Under the right conditions, the "eyes" can sprout and grow new potatoes.

| TOOLS AND EQUIPMENT | Microwave-safe plate | Microwave | 1 to 2 tablespoons olive oil |
|---|---|---|---|
| Large bowl | Paper towels | Pot holder | |
| Chef's knife | Pastry brush | Tongs | 1 teaspoon table salt |
| Cutting board | Measuring spoons | INGREDIENTS | |
| Parchment paper | | 1 russet potato | |

1. Fill a large bowl about halfway with ice, then add cold water to about 2 inches below the top of the bowl.

2. Scrub the potato to remove any dirt from the skin. Potatoes grow in the ground, so make sure you're getting any dirt out of the eyes. Using a knife, cut the potatoes as thin as you can. If possible, the potato slices should be almost transparent. Quickly submerge each potato slice in the ice water. This will keep the potatoes from turning grayish or pink. Let the potato slices soak in the ice water for at least 5 minutes.

3. Place a piece of parchment paper on a microwave-safe plate.

4. Working in batches, remove enough potato slices from the water to cover the plate in a single layer. Leave the remaining potato slices in the water until you are ready to cook them.

5. Use paper towels to dry the potato slices and arrange them on the plate so they are not touching.

Continued on next page

6. Brush each potato slice with a light coating of olive oil and sprinkle lightly with salt. Microwave on high for 2 minutes, 30 seconds.

7. Using oven mitts or pot holders, carefully remove the plate from the microwave.

8. Using tongs, flip the potato chips over.

9. Return the potatoes to the microwave and cook on high for 2 more minutes, or until golden brown. The timing may vary based on your microwave. If the potato chips are not golden brown after 2 minutes, continue to cook in 30-second increments until the potato chips are golden.

10. Sprinkle the chips lightly with salt while still hot.

11. Repeat with the remaining potato slices.

Per serving: Calories: 144; Total fat: 7g; Cholesterol: 0mg; Sodium: 1184mg; Total carbohydrates: 19g; Fiber: 1g; Sugar: 1g; Protein: 2g

## Switch It Up

**GARLIC AND ONION POTATO CHIPS:** Put ¼ teaspoon table salt, ¼ teaspoon garlic powder, and ¼ teaspoon onion powder in a small bowl. Stir to combine. Prepare the recipe as described, except don't salt the potatoes. When the potato chips are removed from the microwave, sprinkle them with the garlic-onion mixture.

**EVERYTHING BAGEL POTATO CHIPS:** Prepare the recipe as described, except don't salt the potatoes. When the potato chips are removed from the microwave, sprinkle them with everything bagel seasoning.

**CINNAMON-SUGAR POTATO CHIPS:** Put 1 teaspoon sugar and ½ teaspoon ground cinnamon in a small bowl. Stir to combine. Prepare the recipe as described, except don't salt the potatoes. When the potato chips are removed from the microwave, sprinkle them with the cinnamon-sugar mixture.

# Maple Granola with Cranberries

**Makes about 6 cups**
**Prep time: 10 minutes / Cook time: 1 hour 15 minutes**

VEGAN  NO DAIRY  NO GLUTEN  **NO SOY**

Once you learn how to make granola at home and realize how cheap and easy it is, you'll never have to buy it again. This recipe calls for raw nuts, but you can use roasted nuts if that's what you have on hand; if you do use roasted nuts, just reserve them until the end so you're not double roasting them in the oven.

**TOOLS AND EQUIPMENT**

*2 rimmed baking sheets*

*Aluminum foil*

*Large bowl*

*Measuring cups*

*Measuring spoons*

*Small bowl*

*Whisk*

*Spatula*

*Pot holder*

*Airtight container*

**INGREDIENTS**

Nonstick cooking spray, for coating the baking sheets

3 cups gluten-free rolled oats

1 cup raw slivered almonds

1 cup raw walnuts

3/4 cup coconut flakes or shredded coconut

1/4 cup plus 2 tablespoons light brown sugar

3 tablespoons ground flaxseed (optional)

1 teaspoon ground cinnamon

3/4 teaspoon table salt

1/4 cup plus 2 tablespoons maple syrup

1/4 cup canola oil, olive oil, or coconut oil

1 teaspoon vanilla extract

1/2 cup dried cranberries

1. Preheat the oven to 250°F.
2. Line 2 rimmed baking sheets with aluminum foil and spray with nonstick cooking spray.
3. In a large bowl, combine the oats, almonds, walnuts, coconut, brown sugar, flaxseed (if using), cinnamon, and salt.

Continued on page 53

4. In a small bowl, combine the maple syrup, canola oil, and vanilla. Whisk together a bit so it's one uniform mixture.

5. Stir the syrup mixture into the oat mixture and keep stirring until the oats are coated. You can use your hands if you think it'll give you a better sense of when the oats are evenly coated.

6. Evenly divide the mixture onto both prepared baking sheets, making sure to spread it into an even layer.

7. Transfer the baking sheets to the oven and bake for about 1 hour 15 minutes, or until the granola looks toasty brown and smells delicious. Stir it using a spatula every 20 minutes as it's baking. Remove from the oven.

8. Evenly divide the dried cranberries between both baking sheets. Using a spatula, press them into the granola mixture.

9. Let the granola cool completely. Break it apart and store it in an airtight container for up to 2 weeks.

**THERE'S SOME LEFT:** You can enjoy this granola on its own, stir it into yogurt, or use it as a topping for the Blueberry-Banana Smoothie Bowl (page 31).

**TRY THIS!** You can use pretty much any dried fruit you like in granola. Just be sure not to put dried fruit in the oven, because it gets too crunchy. Add the fruit after baking, as described in this recipe. If you're feeling extra indulgent, you can add chocolate chips.

Per serving (1/2 cup): Calories: 324; Total fat: 19g; Cholesterol: 0mg; Sodium: 167mg; Total carbohydrates: 36g; Fiber: 5g; Sugar: 18g; Protein: 6g

# Taco Tartlets

**Makes 30 taco bites**
**Prep time: 10 minutes / Cook time: 25 minutes**
NO NUTS

Get all of your favorite taco flavors in a bite-size appetizer. Mini phyllo shells from the freezer section of the grocery store make these tartlets not only very small and cute but also a cinch to assemble.

**TOOLS AND EQUIPMENT**

Chef's knife

Cutting board

Large nonstick skillet

Stirring spoon

Heat-safe bowl

Measuring cup

Measuring spoons

Rimmed baking sheet

Pot holder

......................................

**INGREDIENTS**

1 onion

1 garlic clove

³/₄ pound ground beef

¹/₂ cup prepared taco sauce, such as Ortega taco sauce

¹/₂ teaspoon ground cumin

¹/₄ teaspoon table salt

¹/₈ teaspoon ground black pepper

30 frozen mini phyllo shells

¹/₂ cup shredded Mexican-style cheese blend

1. Preheat the oven to 350°F.
2. Dice the onion by cutting the onion in quarters from root to tip, peeling off the papery outside layers of one of the quarters, and cutting off the tip of the onion, while leaving the root end intact. Cut the onion into tiny cubes.
3. Press the garlic clove so it gets a little squished, then peel off the papery layer and cut off the root end (the nubby side). Mince the garlic: Moving the knife blade in a rocking motion, run the knife over the squished clove repeatedly. Continue this until the garlic is cut into very fine pieces (minced).
4. Heat a large nonstick skillet over medium heat.
5. Once the skillet is hot, add the onion, garlic, and beef. Cook, breaking up the beef into small crumbles and stirring occasionally, for 8 to 10 minutes. Remove from the heat.

6. In order to properly discard the excess fat, you need to drain it off. Push the beef to one side of the pan and slowly tilt the pan, allowing the fat to pool on the other side. Then using a spoon, transfer the fat into a heat-safe bowl. Be sure to use a buffer for your hands or any surfaces when you're moving the bowl of fat—it will be very hot. Set the fat aside to cool; later, when it's cool, scoop it into the trash.

7. Return the skillet to the stove over medium-high heat.

8. Add the taco sauce, cumin, salt, and pepper. Cook, stirring, for 1 to 2 minutes, or until the mixture is heated through. Remove from the heat.

9. Place the frozen phyllo shells on a rimmed baking sheet.

10. Spoon the beef mixture evenly into the shells and top with the shredded cheese.

11. Transfer the baking sheet to the oven and bake for 9 to 10 minutes, or until the shells are crisp and the cheese has melted. Remove from the oven.

12. Add toppings, such as guacamole, sour cream, and sliced olives, as desired.

TRY THIS! You can easily make this recipe meat-free by swapping out the ground beef for canned black beans. Drain the beans and add them in place of the ground beef. If you want a smoother texture, using a fork, mash the beans a bit before adding them to the phyllo shells.

THERE'S SOME LEFT: If you have leftovers, you can easily reheat them in a 300°F oven for 5 minutes or in the microwave for 30 seconds.

Per serving (1 tartlet): Calories: 54; Total fat: 3g; Cholesterol: 12mg; Sodium: 83mg; Total carbohydrates: 3g; Fiber: <1g; Sugar: <1g; Protein: 4g

# Buffalo Cauliflower Bites

**Serves 6**
**Prep time: 10 minutes / Cook time: 30 minutes**
VEGETARIAN NO NUTS

In this recipe, fresh cauliflower florets are coated in a flavored batter and baked until golden, then coated in spicy Buffalo sauce and baked until crispy. Serve them with creamy blue cheese dressing and celery. Fun fact: the "B" is capitalized in Buffalo wings and their spin-offs because the original dish is named after the city of Buffalo, New York.

**TOOLS AND EQUIPMENT**

*Rimmed baking sheet*

*Aluminum foil*

*Chef's knife*

*Cutting board*

*Strainer*

*Measuring cups*

*Measuring spoons*

*Large bowl*

*Whisk*

*Pot holder*

*Tongs*

*Small bowl*

*Pastry brush or folded paper towel*

.................................

**INGREDIENTS**

Nonstick cooking spray, for coating the baking sheet

1 head cauliflower

½ cup all-purpose flour

2 teaspoons garlic powder

1 teaspoon paprika

½ teaspoon table salt

¼ teaspoon ground black pepper

½ cup water

⅔ cup hot sauce, such as Frank's RedHot

1 tablespoon unsalted butter, melted

Celery sticks, carrots, and blue cheese dressing, for serving

1. Preheat the oven to 450°F. Line a rimmed baking sheet with aluminum foil and spray with nonstick cooking spray.

2. Before you wash the cauliflower, cut it into bite-size florets. First, cut the cauliflower in half from the top of the crown down through the middle of the central stem. You'll see all the florets are attached to the core. Use the tip of your knife to cut the florets away from the core, making sure you're not cutting toward yourself. Once all the florets are off the core, you can cut through the little floret stems to make them a little more bite-size. It's easier to wash the cauliflower when it's cut into smaller pieces, so wash the florets in a strainer before you set them aside.

3. Put the flour, garlic powder, paprika, salt, and pepper in a large bowl. Whisk to combine.

4. To make the batter, add the water to the flour mixture and whisk until smooth and lump-free.

5. Add the cauliflower florets to the batter and toss until the florets are completely coated.

6. Place the coated cauliflower in a single layer on the prepared baking sheet.

7. Transfer the baking sheet to the oven and bake for 10 minutes.

8. Remove the baking sheet from the oven. Using tongs, flip the cauliflower over so it cooks evenly.

9. Return the baking sheet to the oven and bake for 10 more minutes.

10. While the cauliflower is baking, put the hot sauce and melted butter in a small bowl and whisk to combine.

11. Once the cauliflower has baked for a total of 20 minutes, remove the baking sheet from the oven again. Brush the cauliflower with the hot sauce mixture, making sure to completely coat each piece.

12. Return the baking sheet to the oven and bake for 10 minutes, or until the cauliflower is crispy and lightly browned. Remove from the oven.

13. Serve the Buffalo cauliflower immediately with celery, carrots, and blue cheese dressing.

TRY THIS! Not a fan of spicy food? You can easily substitute barbecue sauce for the hot sauce.

Per serving: Calories: 84; Total fat: 2g; Cholesterol: 5mg; Sodium: 1086mg; Total carbohydrates: 14g; Fiber: 3g; Sugar: 2g; Protein: 3g

# Peanut Butter and Banana Panini

## Serves 1

**Prep time: 5 minutes / Cook time: 5 minutes**

**VEGETARIAN** **NO SOY** **5 INGREDIENTS OR LESS** **REALLY FAST**

A panini is typically a grilled sandwich that is pressed when cooked. In this sweet version, banana slices drizzled with honey are nestled between layers of creamy peanut butter, and the sandwich is toasted until the bread is crispy and golden brown. A panini pan or press is helpful for this recipe but not necessary.

**TOOLS AND EQUIPMENT**

*Measuring spoons*

*Chef's knife*

*Cutting board*

*Large skillet*

*Heat-safe dinner plate*

......................................

**INGREDIENTS**

4 tablespoons peanut butter

2 bread slices of choice

½ banana, thinly sliced

1 tablespoon honey

2 tablespoons unsalted butter, at room temperature, divided

1. Spread 2 tablespoons of peanut butter on each bread slice.
2. Place the banana pieces in a single layer on the peanut butter on 1 bread slice.
3. Drizzle the honey over the banana slices.
4. Place the other bread slice on top.
5. Spread 1 tablespoon of butter on the outside of the sandwich. It's better if the butter is spread evenly, but it really doesn't have to be perfectly even.
6. Preheat a large skillet over medium-high heat and add the remaining 1 tablespoon of butter.
7. Once the skillet is hot and the butter has fully melted, add the sandwich.

8. Place a heat-safe dinner plate on top of the sandwich to compress it. Cook for 2 minutes, or until the bottom is golden brown.

9. Flip the sandwich, placing the plate back on top and cook the other side for 2 minutes, or until golden brown. Remove from the heat.

**TRY THIS!** Add a layer of chocolate-hazlenut spread on top of the peanut butter layer for a multi-nut sweet treat. You can also swap out the peanut butter for your favorite nut butter.

Per serving: Calories: 936; Total fat: 59g; Cholesterol: 61mg; Sodium: 548mg; Total carbohydrates: 89g; Fiber: 17g; Sugar: 38g; Protein: 27g

# Classic Turkey Club Sandwiches

**Makes 2 sandwiches**
**Prep time: 10 minutes / Cook time: 10 minutes**

NO DAIRY  NO NUTS  FAST

Club sandwiches are probably one of the most iconic American multiple-meat sandwiches. The club has layers of flavors and textures that are easily customizable, and it gives us an opportunity to use the term "double-decker sandwich," which is not a term you get to use every day.

**TOOLS AND EQUIPMENT**

Microwave-safe plate

Paper towels

Microwave

Pot holder

Toaster

Cutting board

Chef's knife

Measuring spoons

8 small skewers or toothpicks

Serrated knife

**INGREDIENTS**

8 bacon slices

6 white bread slices

4 romaine lettuce leaves

1 large tomato

6 tablespoons mayonnaise

8 deli roasted turkey slices

1. Line a large microwave-safe plate with 2 layers of paper towels.

2. Lay 4 bacon slices on the prepared plate. Cover the bacon with another paper towel. Microwave on high for 3 to 4 minutes (depending on the power of your microwave). Using pot holders or oven mitts, carefully remove the plate from the microwave—the plate will be hot.

3. Repeat with the remaining 4 bacon slices.

4. While the bacon is cooking, toast the bread in a toaster.

5. Romaine lettuce leaves are too long for a sandwich, so they need to be cut in half to fit. Lay them on a cutting board and trim off the top ½ inch, removing the limp, darker green part. Trim 1 inch off the bottom, removing the white part. You should be left with the bright green portion of the lettuce leaves. Cut them in half.

Continued on next page

6. Cut the tomato into 8 slices as thick or thin as you prefer.

7. Cut the cooked bacon in half.

8. Arrange 3 toast slices on the cutting board.

9. Spread 1 tablespoon of mayonnaise on each slice.

10. On the first piece of toast, place 2 pieces of lettuce, then 2 tomato slices, 4 pieces of bacon, and 2 turkey slices.

11. Repeat with the second piece of toast.

12. Carefully place the second piece of toast on top of the first with the turkey facing upward, so the arrangement is bread, meat layer, bread, meat layer.

13. Top with the third slice of toast, mayonnaise-side down.

14. Place 1 skewer in each corner of the sandwich going all the way through the bottom, about 1 inch from the edge.

15. Repeat to make 1 more sandwich.

16. Using a serrated knife, cut each sandwich into quarters.

Per serving (1 sandwich): Calories: 763; Total fat: 46g; Cholesterol: 82mg; Sodium: 2045mg; Total carbohydrates: 49g; Fiber: 5g; Sugar: 9g; Protein: 36g

## Switch It Up

**ROAST BEEF CLUB SANDWICH:** Follow directions through step 7. Arrange 3 toast slices on the cutting board. Spread 1 tablespoon prepared horseradish cream sauce on each piece of toast. On the first piece of toast, place 2 pieces of lettuce, 2 tomato slices, 4 pieces of bacon, and 2 deli roast beef slices. Repeat with the second piece of toast. Carefully place the second piece of toast on top of the first with the roast beef facing upward. Top with the third slice of toast, horseradish cream–side down. Continue from step 14.

# Roasted Chicken Salad Pitas

**Makes 4 pitas**
**Prep time: 5 minutes / Cook time: 20 minutes**

"Pita" is the name of a range of flatbreads most common in the Mediterranean and the Middle East, but in this recipe, we're talking about the type of pita that's got a little pocket, which is formed when steam is trapped in the dough as it bakes.

**TOOLS AND EQUIPMENT**

*Large bowl*

*Measuring cups*

*Can opener (if you're using canned chicken)*

*Fine-mesh strainer (if you're using canned chicken)*

*Chef's knife*

*Cutting board*

*Grater*

*Measuring spoons*

*Stirring spoon*

*9-by-9-inch baking dish*

*Pot holder*

....................................

**INGREDIENTS**

3 cups chopped cooked chicken,

or 4 (12½-ounce) cans white chunk chicken

1 celery stalk

4 ounces sharp Cheddar cheese

1 small onion

1 cup mayonnaise

¼ cup slivered almonds

1 teaspoon table salt

1 teaspoon garlic powder

1 teaspoon onion powder

¼ teaspoon ground black pepper

2 cups potato chips

4 pocket pitas

1. Preheat the oven to 450°F.

2. Place the cooked chicken in a large bowl. If you're using canned chicken, drain it in a fine-mesh strainer, then transfer it to the bowl.

3. Cut 1 inch off the top and bottom of the celery stalk. Cut the stalk lengthwise into 4 strips, then cut it crosswise into a fine dice. Keep in mind that you want the pieces small enough that they won't be the only thing you taste in a bite of the sandwich. Add the celery to the bowl.

Continued on next page

4. Using a grater, shred the cheese and add it to the bowl.

5. Finely dice the onion, again keeping in mind how large a piece of raw onion you would want in one bite of sandwich: Start by cutting the onion in half from root to tip. Peel off the papery outside layer and a layer of onion underneath that. For each onion half, cut off the tip of the onion, but leave the root end intact. Cut an onion half in half again from root to tip. Place an onion quarter, flat-side down, on a cutting board. Make several vertical cuts from end to end, being careful not to cut through the root end. Flip the onion quarter onto the other flat side and repeat the vertical cuts, again being careful not to cut through the root end. Then cut the onion crosswise into small, even dice—the pieces should just fall off the knife ready to go. Measure out 2 teaspoons of the diced onion and add to the bowl. Store any leftover onion.

6. Add the mayonnaise, almonds, salt, garlic powder, onion powder, and pepper to the bowl. Stir until everything is completely combined. Transfer to a 9-by-9-inch baking dish.

7. Using your hands, crush the potato chips into small pieces, then sprinkle over the chicken mixture.

8. Transfer the baking dish to the oven and roast for 15 to 20 minutes, or until the mixture is hot and bubbly. Remove from the oven.

9. Serve the chicken salad in pitas, which you can toast very briefly if you want to warm them up.

**THERE'S SOME LEFT:** For a light leftover lunch, the chicken salad can be served on top of mixed salad greens or wrapped in a lettuce leaf for a grain-free option.

Per serving (1 pita): Calories: 888; Total fat: 61g; Cholesterol: 109mg; Sodium: 2059mg; Total carbohydrates: 46g; Fiber: 3g; Sugar: 4g; Protein: 39g

# Steak and Cheese Hand Pies

**Makes 6 pies**
**Prep time: 10 minutes / Cook time: 15 minutes**

NO NUTS

These tender and soft treats are filled with creamy cheeses (yes, plural) and hearty beef. Using premade crescent roll dough makes this recipe very easy, but when you have more confidence in the kitchen, you may want to try homemade dough.

**TOOLS AND EQUIPMENT**

*Rimmed baking sheet*

*Parchment paper*

*Measuring spoons*

*Chef's knife*

*Cutting board*

*Fork*

*Small bowl*

*Pastry brush or folded paper towel*

*Pot holder*

**INGREDIENTS**

3 tablespoons onion and chive cream cheese spread or regular cream cheese

1 (8-ounce) can crescent rolls

12 deli roast beef slices

3 provolone cheese slices

3 Cheddar cheese slices

1 large egg

1 tablespoon water

1 teaspoon dried oregano

1. Preheat the oven to 375°F. Line a rimmed baking sheet with parchment paper.

2. If you're using regular cream cheese for this recipe, measure out the amount you're using and leave it on a plate or in a bowl on the counter for 15 minutes or so until it gets a little soft and easier to spread. If you're using a cream cheese spread, that should already be spreadable enough.

3. Unroll the crescent roll dough. Instead of tearing at the perforated seams, squish them together with your fingers so that you have a seamless piece of dough. Cut the dough lengthwise down the center and then cut cross-wise into thirds. You should have 6 squares.

Continued on next page

4. Spread 1½ teaspoons of cream cheese spread on each dough square. Leave a ¼-inch border around the edges.

5. Place 2 deli roast beef slices on top of the cream cheese, making sure to leave a ¼-inch border around the edges.

6. Top each square with ½ provolone cheese slice and ½ Cheddar cheese slice. You may need to cut them smaller to make them fit.

7. Fold each square into a triangle. Using the tips of the tines of a fork, press down semi-firmly on the edges, so that you're making little indentations in the edges to seal the filling in the dough (this is called "crimping," which is related to the Dutch word for "wrinkle").

8. Transfer the hand pies to the prepared baking sheet.

9. Put the egg and water in a small bowl. Using a fork, mix until fully combined and the mixture is minimally streaky. Brush the mixture—which in this context is called egg wash—on top of each hand pie. An egg wash can help seal a baked good, but in this case, you're using it to make the pies look shiny and golden brown.

10. Sprinkle the oregano on top of each hand pie, crushing it a little between your fingers as you sprinkle. Crushing the herbs like this makes them finer and releases more fragrant oils.

11. Transfer the baking sheet to the oven and bake for 14 minutes, or until the dough is golden brown and cooked through. Remove from the oven.

12. Let the pies cool for at least 10 minutes before serving.

Per serving (1 pie): Calories: 290; Total fat: 18g; Cholesterol: 72mg; Sodium: 982mg; Total carbohydrates: 17g; Fiber: <1g; Sugar: 7g; Protein: 16g

## Switch It Up

**PEPPERONI PIZZA HAND PIES:** Prepare the crescent dough as described. Spoon 1 teaspoon prepared marinara sauce onto each dough square, leaving a ¼-inch border around the edges. Place 4 pepperoni slices on top of the marinara, making sure to leave a ¼-inch border around the edges. Top each square with 1 slice of mozzarella cheese cut to fit the dough. Fold each square into a triangle, and using a fork, crimp the edges to seal. Transfer the hand pies to a rimmed baking sheet lined with parchment paper. In a small bowl, combine the egg and water, and using a fork, mix until fully combined. Then brush the egg wash on top of each hand pie. Sprinkle dried Italian seasoning on top. Bake for 14 minutes, or until the dough is golden brown and cooked through.

# Ham and Cheese Pinwheels

**Makes 12 pinwheels**
**Prep time: 10 minutes / Cook time: 25 minutes**
**NO NUTS**

To ensure even baking on these pinwheels, be sure to cut them the same size. If the pinwheels start to brown too much before they're cooked through, cover them loosely with aluminum foil in the oven. You may want to serve these alongside Broccoli-Cheddar Soup (page 104).

**TOOLS AND EQUIPMENT**

*13-by-9-inch baking dish*

*Cutting board*

*Chef's knife*

*Small saucepan or microwave-safe bowl*

*Pot holder*

*Small bowl*

*Measuring spoons*

*Whisk*

**INGREDIENTS**

Nonstick cooking spray, for coating the baking dish

1 (13.8-ounce) tube refrigerated pizza dough

3/4 pound very thinly sliced deli ham

8 ounces very thinly sliced Swiss cheese

8 tablespoons (1 stick) unsalted butter

2 tablespoons honey

1 tablespoon Dijon mustard

2 tablespoons sesame seeds

1. Preheat the oven to 350°F. Spray a 13-by-9-inch baking dish with nonstick cooking spray.
2. Unroll the pizza dough onto a cutting board. Lightly press it into a 13-by-8-inch rectangle.
3. Place the ham on top of the dough, overlapping the slices, to completely cover the dough. Start with a single layer of ham, but if you have extra ham, you can make multiple layers.
4. Layer the cheese on top of the ham using the same technique.
5. Starting on one of the long edges, tightly roll the dough into a log. Pinch the ends to seal them.
6. Cut the dough log in half crosswise to reveal the spiral of dough and filling. Cut each half in half again. Then cut each quarter into 3 even pieces. You should have a total of 12 pinwheels.
7. Arrange the pinwheels in the prepared baking dish.

8. Melt the butter, either in the microwave or in a small saucepan on the stove. If you're melting it in the microwave, put it in a microwave-safe bowl, and microwave in 20-second blasts until it's done. Use hot pads to handle the hot bowl.

9. Put the butter, honey, mustard, and sesame seeds in a small bowl. Whisk to combine. You want this to be a pretty smooth consistency, so put some elbow grease into the whisking, because it can be a little tricky to whisk honey into a sauce or dressing.

10. Pour the butter mixture evenly over the pinwheels.

11. Transfer the baking dish to the oven and bake for 25 minutes, or until golden brown. Remove from the oven.

Per serving (1 pinwheel): Calories: 279; Total fat: 17g; Cholesterol: 50mg; Sodium: 671mg; Total carbohydrates: 21g; Fiber: 1g; Sugar: 5g; Protein: 12g

## Switch It Up

**TURKEY AND CHEESE PINWHEELS:** Prepare the recipe as described, substituting deli turkey for the ham and American cheese for the Swiss cheese. Add ½ cup dried cranberries on top of the cheese before rolling the dough up.

**ITALIAN SUB PINWHEELS:** Prepare the recipe as described, substituting ¼ pound Genoa salami, ¼ pound capocollo or prosciutto, and ¼ pound pepperoni for the ham. Substitute provolone cheese for the Swiss cheese. For the sauce, combine 8 tablespoons melted butter, 1 tablespoon red wine vinegar, and 2 teaspoons Italian seasoning. Pour over the pinwheels.

# Chapter 4
# Salads and Meat-Free Meals

Apple, Walnut, and Cranberry Salad 72

Green Goddess Chopped Salad 74

Deconstructed Spicy-Tangy Elote Salad 76

Fruit Salad with Honey-Citrus Dressing 78

Southwest Quinoa Salad 80

Mediterranean Chickpea Salad 82

Classic Mac and Cheese 84

Spaghetti Marinara 86

Pasta Primavera 89

Baked Creamy Spinach Ravioli 91

Veggie Stir-Fry 93

Vegetarian Miso Ramen 95

Oven-Baked Risotto with Peas 98

Cauliflower Parmesan 99

Stuffed Portabella Mushrooms 101

Broccoli-Cheddar Soup 104

Cheesy Potato Soup 106

# Apple, Walnut, and Cranberry Salad

**Serves 2**

**Prep time: 5 minutes / Cook time: 10 minutes**

**VEGETARIAN  NO GLUTEN  NO SOY  FAST**

Most American walnuts are grown in California, and they're generally harvested using big mechanical shakers that jiggle trees until the walnuts fall out of them. Cranberries, by contrast, grow in bogs or marshes. Farmers harvest them by flooding their bogs and then stirring up the bushes so that the berries are dislodged and float to the surface of the water.

## TOOLS AND EQUIPMENT

*Rimmed baking sheet*

*Stirring spoon*

*Pot holder*

*Chef's knife*

*Cutting board*

*Large bowl*

*Tongs (optional)*

*Measuring cups*

*Measuring spoons*

*Jar with a tight-fitting lid, or whisk and small bowl*

.......................................

## INGREDIENTS

### FOR THE SALAD

1/2 cup raw or toasted walnuts

1 red apple

3 cups mixed field greens

1/4 cup dried cranberries

2 tablespoons crumbled Gorgonzola cheese

### FOR THE DRESSING

2 tablespoons olive oil

2 tablespoons apple cider vinegar

1 tablespoon honey

1/4 teaspoon Dijon mustard

1/8 teaspoon onion powder

1/8 teaspoon garlic powder

1/8 teaspoon ground black pepper

## TO MAKE THE SALAD

1. If the walnuts are already toasted, you can skip right to step 4. If the walnuts are raw, preheat the oven to 350°F.

2. Spread the walnuts out on a rimmed baking sheet, making sure they are in a single layer.

3. Transfer the baking sheet to the oven and bake for 8 minutes, or until the walnuts are lightly toasted. When they're done, they should smell toasty but not burned. Check them after 5 minutes to make sure they're not burning and stir them around. Remove from the oven and set aside to cool.

4. Meanwhile, remove the core from the apple: Place the apple upright on a cutting board and cut off 2 parallel sides of the apple, cutting as close to the core as possible. Cut off the remaining 2 sides, leaving a rectangular-shaped core. Discard the core and cut the apple into thin slices.

5. In a large bowl, using tongs or your hands, combine the field greens, apple, cranberries, and cheese.

6. If you toasted the walnuts in the oven, make sure they've cooled off. Coarsely break them apart using your hands, or cut them using a knife and add them to the salad mixture. Toss to combine.

### TO MAKE THE DRESSING

7. Put the olive oil, vinegar, honey, mustard, onion powder, garlic powder, and pepper into a jar with a tight-fitting lid.

8. Shake the jar until the dressing is completely combined. Making the dressing in a jar is an easy way to ensure it is fully emulsified, but you can also simply whisk the ingredients in a small bowl.

9. Pour the dressing over the salad and toss so everything is evenly coated. Serve immediately.

**DON'T HAVE IT?** If you don't have apple cider vinegar, use distilled white vinegar or balsamic vinegar.

Per serving: Calories: 502; Total fat: 36g; Cholesterol: 6mg; Sodium: 140mg; Total carbohydrates: 45g; Fiber: 7g; Sugar: 34g; Protein: 8g

# Green Goddess Chopped Salad

### Serves 2
### Prep time: 10 minutes

VEGETARIAN NO GLUTEN NO HEAT NECESSARY REALLY FAST

This salad is packed with good-for-you ingredients, such as avocado. Avocado has an enzyme in it that browns when it's exposed to oxygen, so save the half with the pit in it (combined with, hopefully, a reusable plastic cover) to help lessen the exposure to air.

**TOOLS AND EQUIPMENT**

*Large bowl*

*Measuring cups*

*Chef's knife*

*Cutting board*

*Measuring spoons*

*Food processor or blender*

*Tongs*

**INGREDIENTS**

**FOR THE SALAD**

2 cups packed baby spinach

1 cup arugula

1 ripe avocado

1 red onion

¼ cup crumbled feta cheese

**FOR THE DRESSING**

½ cup plain Greek yogurt

¼ cup mayonnaise

1 cup basil leaves

1 scallion

1 tablespoon prepared basil pesto

2 tablespoons apple cider vinegar

2 teaspoons honey

½ teaspoon Dijon mustard

⅛ teaspoon table salt

Pinch ground black pepper

**TO MAKE THE SALAD**

1. Put the spinach and arugula in a large bowl.

2. Using a chef's knife, cut the avocado lengthwise, maneuvering your knife around the pit. Firmly grip both sides of the avocado and twist around the pit to separate the halves. Tightly wrap the half with the pit in it and store for another use (perhaps the Everything Bagel Avocado Toast on page 22). Using a spoon, scoop along the avocado skin to remove the flesh. Cut into 1-inch chunks and add to the bowl.

3. Cut the onion in half from root to tip. Peel off the papery outside layer and a layer of onion underneath that. Place an onion half, flat-side down, on a cutting board. Cut off the tip of the onion, but leave the root end intact. Then, cut the onion into thin slices, so that the layers of the onion come apart into little crescents for your salad. Discard the root end. Add ⅛ cup of sliced onion to the bowl, pulling apart the layers as you do so and store any leftover onion.

4. Add the cheese to the bowl.

**TO MAKE THE DRESSING**

5. In a food processor or blender, combine the yogurt, mayonnaise, basil, scallion, pesto, vinegar, honey, mustard, salt, and pepper. Process on high speed until you get your desired consistency.

6. Pour the dressing over the salad. Using tongs, toss the salad.

**TRY THIS!** You can easily turn this salad into a heartier meal by adding your favorite cooked protein. Toss in some chicken, tuna, or a hard-boiled egg (page 21).

Per serving: Calories: 440; Total fat: 37g; Cholesterol: 48mg; Sodium: 715mg; Total carbohydrates: 16g; Fiber: 4g; Sugar: 10g; Protein: 13g

# Deconstructed Spicy-Tangy Elote Salad

### Serves 2
### Prep time: 10 minutes / Cook time: 15 minutes
**VEGETARIAN NO GLUTEN NO NUTS**

Elote is a beloved Latin American street food in which a corn cob is typically slathered in mayonnaise, margarine, lime juice, cheese, and spices. Here, you won't get the thrill of buying food from a cart, but you can still get all of the flavors of elote served as a salad.

**TOOLS AND EQUIPMENT**

*Cutting board*

*Chef's knife*

*Large skillet*

*Measuring cups*

*Measuring spoons*

*Stirring spoon*

*Large bowl*

*Small bowl*

*Whisk*

..................................

**INGREDIENTS**

1 red onion

1 garlic clove

1 tablespoon unsalted butter

2 cups frozen corn, thawed

1 tablespoon mayonnaise

1 tablespoon sour cream

Juice of ½ lime

1 teaspoon table salt

¼ teaspoon chili powder

¼ teaspoon ground black pepper

2 tablespoons queso fresco

2 tablespoons finely chopped fresh cilantro

1. To finely dice the onion, start by cutting the onion in half from root to tip. Peel off the papery outside layer and a layer of onion underneath that. For each onion half, cut off the tip of the onion, but leave the root end intact. Cut an onion half in half again from root to tip. Place an onion quarter, flat-side down, on a cutting board. Make several vertical cuts from end to end, being careful not to cut through the root end. Flip the onion quarter onto the other flat side, and repeat the vertical cuts, again being careful not to cut through the root end. Then cut the onion crosswise into small, even dice—the pieces should just fall off the knife ready to go. Set aside ¼ onion and store any leftover onion.

2. Press the garlic clove so it gets a little squished, then peel off the papery layer and cut off the root end (the nubby side). Mince the garlic: Moving the knife blade in a rocking motion, run the knife over the squished clove repeatedly. Use the knife blade to turn the pile of cut garlic a quarter turn every few seconds. Continue this until the garlic is cut into very fine pieces (minced).

3. In a large skillet, melt the butter over medium-high heat.

4. Add the corn and cook for about 10 minutes, or until golden and slightly charred. Transfer to a large bowl.

5. Add the onion to the skillet and cook for 2 to 3 minutes, or until the onion is softened and fragrant.

6. Add the garlic and cook for about 30 seconds. Remove from the heat.

7. Transfer the onion and garlic to the bowl with the corn.

8. To make the dressing, put the mayonnaise, sour cream, lime juice, salt, chili powder, and pepper in a small bowl. Whisk until combined.

9. Pour the dressing over the corn mixture and stir to combine.

10. Add the queso fresco and cilantro and stir.

**DON'T HAVE IT?** If you don't have queso fresco, you can substitute Cotija cheese or even feta, which has a similar texture when you crumble it.

Per serving: Calories: 306; Total fat: 17g; Cholesterol: 34mg; Sodium: 1360mg; Total carbohydrates: 36g; Fiber: 4g; Sugar: 7g; Protein: 8g

# Fruit Salad with Honey-Citrus Dressing

### Serves 2
### Prep time: 10 minutes

VEGETARIAN  NO DAIRY  NO GLUTEN  **NO SOY**  NO NUTS
NO HEAT NECESSARY  REALLY FAST

If you don't have time to chop the fruit for this salad, note that you can often find chopped fresh fruit in the produce department of the grocery store.

**TOOLS AND EQUIPMENT**

*Chef's knife*

*Cutting board*

*Large bowl*

*Measuring cups*

*Spoon*

*Stirring spoon*

*Measuring spoons*

*Small bowl*

*Whisk*

**INGREDIENTS**

1 apple (any variety)

1 cup strawberries

1 cup red grapes

1 kiwi

1 orange

1 banana

1 cup blueberries

2 tablespoons honey

2 tablespoons orange juice

1 tablespoon lemon juice

1. Peel the apple if you prefer a peeled apple, then remove the core: Place the apple upright on a cutting board and cut off 2 parallel sides of the apple, cutting as close to the core as possible. Cut off the remaining 2 sides, leaving a rectangular-shaped core. Discard the core. Cut the apple into bite-size pieces and transfer to a large bowl.

2. Remove the hulls from the strawberries, cut them into bite-size pieces, then add to the bowl.

3. Cut the grapes in half whichever way you like and add to the bowl.

4. Cut the kiwi in half, and using a spoon, gently scoop the flesh out of the skin. Cut into bite-size pieces and add to the bowl.

5. Peel the orange and separate the segments. Cut into bite-size pieces and add to the bowl.

6. Peel and slice the banana and add to the bowl.

7. Add the blueberries to the bowl. Gently stir the fruit together.

8. To make the dressing, put the honey, orange juice, and lemon juice in a small bowl. Whisk vigorously until the honey is fully combined into the juices.

9. Pour the dressing over the fruit and stir to combine.

Per serving: Calories: 301; Total fat: 1g; Cholesterol: 0mg; Sodium: 6mg; Total carbohydrates: 78g; Fiber: 9g; Sugar: 60g; Protein: 3g

## Switch It Up

**TROPICAL FRUIT SALAD:** Substitute 1 cup chopped pineapple for the apple and substitute 1 cup chopped mango for the grapes. Prepare the rest of the recipe as instructed.

**FRUIT SALAD WITH MINT DRESSING:** Prepare the fruit as instructed. For the mint dressing, put 1 tablespoon finely chopped mint in a small bowl. Use the handle of a wooden spoon to crush the mint to release its natural oils. Add the juice of 1 orange, the juice of 2 limes, and 1 teaspoon honey. Stir to combine and pour over the chopped fruit.

**MELON SALAD:** Substitute 1 cup chopped honeydew for the apple, substitute 1 cup chopped cantaloupe for the grapes, and substitute 1 cup chopped watermelon for the blueberries. Prepare the rest of the recipe as instructed.

# Southwest Quinoa Salad

### Serves 3 or 4
### Prep time: 15 minutes / Cook time: 20 minutes

**VEGETARIAN** NO GLUTEN **NO SOY** NO NUTS

Quinoa is a flowering plant that hails from the Andes. The quinoa we eat is actually the seeds of the plant. I often make a double batch of quinoa and freeze half for later use. If you use frozen quinoa in this salad, just make sure to leave it in the fridge until it thaws before using.

**TOOLS AND EQUIPMENT**

*Measuring cups*

*Fine-mesh strainer*

*Small saucepan*

*Can opener*

*Measuring spoons*

*Large bowl*

*Chef's knife*

*Cutting board*

*Spoon*

*Fork*

*Stirring spoon*

**INGREDIENTS**

½ cup quinoa (any variety)

1 cup vegetable broth

¾ cup canned black beans

½ cup canned corn

1 red bell pepper

1 red onion

1 ripe avocado

2 tablespoons chopped fresh cilantro

¼ cup prepared cilantro-lime salad dressing, such as Briannas Fine Salad Dressings

1. If you're using precooked quinoa, skip to step 4. If you're using uncooked quinoa, rinse it with cool water before you cook it. Put the uncooked quinoa in a fine-mesh strainer and let water run over it in the sink for 30 seconds to 1 minute. Use your hands to move the quinoa around as the water is running over it. Put the rinsed quinoa in a small saucepan.

2. Add the vegetable broth. Bring to a boil over high heat.

3. Reduce the heat to a simmer. Cover the pan and simmer for 15 minutes, or until all of the liquid is absorbed—just let it be and don't remove the lid. Remove from the heat. Let stand, covered, for at least 5 minutes. Do not peek inside the pan.

4. While the quinoa is cooking, drain the black beans and corn in a strainer, then rinse with cold water. Put the beans and corn in a large bowl.

5. Cut the bell pepper in half, and using your hands, remove the seeds, white membranes, and stem. Chop half of the bell pepper into small pieces and add to the bowl. Wrap the remaining half of the bell pepper and store for another use (check out the Mediterranean Chickpea Salad on page 82).

6. Cut the onion in half from root to tip. Peel off the papery outside layer and a layer of onion underneath that. Place an onion half, flat-side down, on a cutting board. Cut off the tip of the onion, but leave the root end intact. Then, cut the onion into thin slices, so that the layers of the onion come apart into little crescents for your salad. Discard the root end. Add ¼ cup of sliced onion to the bowl, pulling apart the layers as you do so and store any leftover onion.

7. Using a chef's knife, cut the avocado lengthwise, maneuvering your knife around the pit. Firmly grip both sides of the avocado and twist around the pit to separate the halves. Tightly wrap the half with the pit in it and store for another use (check out the Green Goddess Chopped Salad on page 74). Using a spoon, scoop along the avocado skin to remove the flesh. Cut into ½-inch chunks and add to the bowl.

8. Add the cilantro to the bowl.

9. Using a fork, fluff the quinoa, then transfer to the bowl. Gently stir all the salad ingredients together.

10. Pour the dressing over the salad and stir until it's evenly distributed.

**THERE'S SOME LEFT:** This salad is great served warm or cold. If you have leftover Southwest Quinoa Salad, serve it over your favorite greens, or toss in some cooked chicken or canned tuna for added protein.

Per serving: Calories: 339; Total fat: 16g; Cholesterol: 7mg; Sodium: 570mg; Total carbohydrates: 41g; Fiber: 9g; Sugar: 7g; Protein: 9g

# Mediterranean Chickpea Salad

### Serves 2
### Prep time: 10 minutes

VEGAN  NO DAIRY  NO GLUTEN  **NO SOY**  NO NUTS  NO HEAT NECESSARY  REALLY FAST

Chickpeas, also referred to as garbanzo beans, grow in little green pods on a bushy smallish plant. Chickpeas are a high-protein legume that shine in this bright vegetarian salad, which is delicious served in a pita. It's a hearty, meatless meal that's very filling.

**TOOLS AND EQUIPMENT**

*Can opener*

*Strainer*

*Large bowl*

*Chef's knife*

*Cutting board*

*Peeler*

*Small bowl*

*Measuring cups*

*Measuring spoons*

*Whisk*

......................................

**INGREDIENTS**

1 (15½-ounce) can chickpeas

1 red bell pepper

½ cucumber

¾ cup chopped fresh parsley

1 red onion

1½ tablespoons olive oil

1½ tablespoons lemon juice

¼ teaspoon garlic powder

¼ teaspoon table salt

¼ teaspoon ground black pepper

1. Drain the chickpeas in a strainer, then rinse with cold water. Transfer to a large bowl.

2. Cut the bell pepper in half and using your hands, remove the seeds, white membranes, and stem. Chop half of the bell pepper into small pieces and add to the bowl. Wrap the remaining half of the bell pepper and store for another use (check out the Southwest Quinoa Salad on page 80).

3. Peel the cucumber and chop ¼ inch off of each end. Cut into ¼-inch pieces and add to the bowl.

4. Add the parsley to the bowl.

5. To finely dice the onion, start by cutting the onion in half from root to tip. Peel off the papery outside layer and a layer of onion underneath that. For each onion half, cut off the tip of the onion, but leave the root end intact. Cut an onion half in half again from root to tip. Place an onion quarter, flat-side down, on a cutting board. Make several vertical cuts from end to end, being careful not to cut through the root end. Flip the onion quarter onto the other flat side and repeat the vertical cuts, again being careful not to cut through the root end. Then cut the onion crosswise into small, even dice—the pieces should just fall off the knife ready to go. Add ¼ cup of onion pieces to the bowl and store any leftover onion.

6. To make the dressing, in a small bowl, combine the olive oil, lemon juice, garlic powder, salt, and pepper. Whisk together.

7. Pour the dressing over the salad and mix until the salad is completely combined.

**TRY THIS!** Kick up the Mediterranean flavor by adding ¼ cup crumbled feta cheese and ¼ cup chopped Kalamata olives.

Per serving: Calories: 327; Total fat: 15g; Cholesterol: 0mg; Sodium: 664mg; Total carbohydrates: 41g; Fiber: 12g; Sugar: 10g; Protein: 12g

# Classic Mac and Cheese

**Serves 2**

**Prep time: 5 minutes / Cook time: 20 minutes**

**VEGETARIAN  NO SOY  NO NUTS**

Macaroni and cheese is surprisingly easy to make from scratch! In commercial production of the elbow macaroni (the pasta Americans typically associate with the word "macaroni"), the dough is squeezed through a mold and then cut into little pieces when it pops out the other side as a little raw pasta tube.

| TOOLS AND EQUIPMENT | *Medium saucepan* | 8 ounces elbow macaroni | ¼ teaspoon table salt |
|---|---|---|---|
| *Large pot* | *Measuring spoons* | 1 cup milk | ⅛ teaspoon ground black pepper |
| *Heat-safe bowl* | *Whisk* | 2 tablespoons unsalted butter | |
| *Measuring cups* | | 2 tablespoons all-purpose flour | 1 cup shredded Cheddar cheese |
| *Strainer* | INGREDIENTS | | |
| *Small saucepan* | Salt, for cooking the macaroni | | |

1. Bring a large pot of salted water to a boil over high heat.

2. Add the macaroni and cook according to the package directions, usually about 7 minutes, until tender. Remove from the heat. Reserve 2 cups of the cooking water in a heat-safe bowl in case you need to use it later. Drain the macaroni in a strainer.

3. Pour the milk into a small saucepan and gently warm over low heat. Milk burns pretty easily, so make sure the heat is low and you're keeping an eye on it, stirring at least every minute or so. The milk doesn't have to be scalding hot or boiling, just warmed up.

4. While the milk warms, in a medium saucepan or skillet, melt the butter over medium-high heat.

5. Whisk in the flour and cook, stirring constantly as a paste forms, for 3 to 5 minutes. The paste should turn a little brown. The paste is called a roux (pronounced as in "kangaroo"), and it is a thickener made when you brown flour and some type of fat (in this case butter).

6. Very slowly whisk in the warmed milk, a little bit at a time, making sure the roux you made is being incorporated and not just clumping up.

7. Add the salt and pepper.

8. Once the mixture is warm and bubbling a little, stir in ½ cup of cheese and whisk until combined.

9. Stir in the remaining ½ cup of cheese and whisk until completely melted.

10. Reduce the heat to low. Add the cooked macaroni. If the mixture is too thick, you can add the reserved pasta water, ¼ cup at a time, stirring after each addition, until you reach the desired consistency. Stir until all of the macaroni is completely covered in the cheese sauce. Remove from the heat and serve.

Per serving: Calories: 832; Total fat: 33g; Cholesterol: 93mg; Sodium: 726mg; Total carbohydrates: 99g; Fiber: 4g; Sugar: 10g; Protein: 33g

## Switch It Up

**BUFFALO CHICKEN:** Drain a 5-ounce can of chicken and put it in a large skillet. Stir in 1 to 2 tablespoons of Buffalo sauce and cook for 2 minutes. Remove the chicken from the skillet and add it to the cheese sauce along with ½ cup blue cheese crumbles before adding the pasta. Prepare the rest of the recipe as instructed.

# Spaghetti Marinara

**Serves 2**

**Prep time: 10 minutes / Cook time: 30 minutes**

VEGETARIAN **NO SOY** NO NUTS

This sauce is quick, but it tastes like it was simmered all day. The secret is the bay leaf—an aromatic leaf from laurel trees or bay trees. Bay leaves are dried, and they release their aromatic essential oils when you cook them in your food. Don't skip them!

**TOOLS AND EQUIPMENT**

*Chef's knife*

*Cutting board*

*Medium saucepan*

*Measuring spoons*

*Stirring spoon*

*Can opener*

*Large pot*

*Strainer*

....................................

**INGREDIENTS**

1 onion

1 garlic clove

1 tablespoon olive oil

½ teaspoon dried oregano

½ teaspoon dried basil

1 (15-ounce) can crushed tomatoes

1 bay leaf

¼ teaspoon table salt

⅛ teaspoon ground black pepper

8 ounces of your favorite pasta

2 tablespoons grated vegetarian parmesan cheese

1. To finely dice the onion, start by cutting the onion in half from root to tip. Peel off the papery outside layer and a layer of onion underneath that. For each onion half, cut off the tip of the onion, but leave the root end intact. Cut an onion half in half again from root to tip. Place an onion quarter, flat-side down, on a cutting board. Make several vertical cuts from end to end, being careful not to cut through the root end. Flip the onion quarter onto the other flat side and repeat the vertical cuts, again being careful not to cut through the root end. Then cut the onion crosswise into small, even dice—the pieces should just fall off the knife ready to go. Set aside ¼ onion and store any leftover onion.

2. Press the garlic clove so it gets a little squished, then peel off the papery layer, and cut off the root end (the nubby side). Mince the garlic: Moving the knife blade in a rocking motion, run the knife over the squished clove repeatedly. Use the knife blade to turn the pile of cut garlic a quarter turn every few seconds. Continue this until the garlic is cut into very fine pieces (minced).

3. In a medium saucepan, heat the olive oil over medium heat.

4. Once the olive oil is hot, add the onion, oregano, and basil. Cook, stirring occasionally, for about 5 minutes, or until the onion is translucent.

5. Add the garlic and stir for 30 seconds, or until the garlic is fragrant.

6. Add the crushed tomatoes, bay leaf, salt, and pepper.

7. Reduce the heat to medium-low. Simmer for 20 minutes. Remove from the heat.

8. Meanwhile, bring a large pot of salted water to a boil over high heat.

9. Add the pasta to the boiling water and cook according to the package directions, usually about 10 minutes, until tender. Remove from the heat. Drain the pasta in a strainer and return to the large pot.

10. When the sauce is finished, carefully remove the bay leaf and discard.

11. Pour the sauce into the large pot with the pasta and toss to combine.

12. Serve the pasta topped with the parmesan cheese.

OOPS . . . If your sauce gets too thick, you can thin it with some of the pasta water, which is infused with the pasta starch. Before draining your pasta, reserve 1 cup of the cooking water, pour a little bit of the water into your sauce, and briefly simmer, if needed. The nice thing about adding water to a sauce is that even if you accidentally add too much, you can just cook it off a little until the sauce reaches your desired consistency.

Per serving: Calories: 586; Total fat: 11g; Cholesterol: 5mg; Sodium: 809mg; Total carbohydrates: 104g; Fiber: 8g; Sugar: 13g; Protein: 20g

# Pasta Primavera

### Serves 2
### Prep time: 5 minutes / Cook time: 25 minutes

VEGETARIAN **NO SOY** NO NUTS

"Primavera" means "spring" in Italian, and the decadent and creamy vegetable primavera sauce in this recipe certainly features a lot of bright spring colors. After you thaw the vegetables, it's important to drain the excess water from them so they don't water the sauce down.

**TOOLS AND EQUIPMENT**

*Large saucepan or pot*

*Measuring cups*

*Strainer*

*Chef's knife*

*Cutting board*

*Large skillet*

*Measuring spoons*

*Stirring spoon*

........................................

**INGREDIENTS**

1 cup spiral pasta

1 onion

1 garlic clove

1 tablespoon unsalted butter

1 (8-ounce) package mixed frozen vegetables (look for broccoli, cauliflower, and carrots), thawed

2/3 cup heavy cream

2/3 cup grated vegetarian parmesan cheese

1/2 teaspoon table salt

1/8 teaspoon ground black pepper

1. Bring a large saucepan or pot of water to a boil over high heat.

2. Add the pasta and cook according to the package directions, usually 8 to 12 minutes, until tender. Remove from the heat. Drain in a strainer.

3. Meanwhile, to finely dice the onion, start by cutting the onion in half from root to tip. Peel off the papery outside layer and a layer of onion underneath that. For each onion half, cut off the tip of the onion, but leave the root end intact. Cut an onion half in half again from root to tip. Place an onion quarter, flat-side down, on a cutting board. Make several vertical cuts from end to end, being careful not to cut through the root end. Flip the onion quarter onto the other flat side and repeat the vertical cuts, again being careful not to cut through the root end. Then cut the onion crosswise into small, even dice—the pieces should just fall off the knife ready to go. Set aside 1/4 onion and store any leftover onion.

Continued on next page

4. Press the garlic clove so it gets a little squished, then peel off the papery layer and cut off the root end (the nubby side). Mince the garlic: Moving the knife blade in a rocking motion, run the knife over the squished clove repeatedly. Use the knife blade to turn the pile of cut garlic a quarter turn every few seconds. Continue this until the garlic is cut into very fine pieces (minced).

5. In a large skillet, melt the butter over medium-high heat.

6. Add the onion and cook for 5 minutes, or until the onion is translucent.

7. Add the garlic and cook for 30 more seconds.

8. Drain any excess water from the thawed vegetables and add the vegetables and heavy cream.

9. Reduce the heat to low. Simmer for 10 minutes, or until the vegetables are tender.

10. Add the cooked pasta, parmesan cheese, salt, and pepper. Stir until thoroughly combined and heated through. Remove from the heat.

OOPS . . . Forgot to thaw the vegetables? No problem! Simply place the frozen vegetables in a microwave-safe bowl and cover with a microwave-safe plate. Microwave on high for 3 to 4 minutes, checking the vegetables about halfway through the cooking time. Once the vegetables are thawed, drain any excess water and add them to the dish.

Per serving: Calories: 724; Total fat: 45g; Cholesterol: 132mg; Sodium: 1264mg; Total carbohydrates: 60g; Fiber: 6g; Sugar: 4g; Protein: 22g

# Baked Creamy Spinach Ravioli

### Serves 4
### Prep time: 10 minutes / Cook time: 30 minutes
**VEGETARIAN NO SOY NO NUTS**

Ravioli is often described as a "pasta envelope," which is a fun fact for you to break out when you're serving this dish. Please note that when you're making the cream sauce in this recipe, it's important that you slowly and steadily whisk in the milk and cream to avoid lumps forming.

**TOOLS AND EQUIPMENT**

*Chef's knife*

*Cutting board*

*Large oven-safe skillet*

*Stirring spoon*

*Measuring spoons*

*Measuring cups*

*Whisk*

*Pot holder*

......................................

**INGREDIENTS**

1 onion

3 garlic cloves

7 ounces baby spinach

1 tablespoon olive oil

1 tablespoon all-purpose flour

1 cup heavy cream

½ cup milk

½ cup grated vegetarian parmesan cheese

1 teaspoon table salt

½ teaspoon ground black pepper

1 (16-ounce) package frozen cheese ravioli, thawed

1 cup shredded mozzarella cheese

1. Preheat the oven to 375°F.
2. To finely dice the onion, start by cutting the onion in half from root to tip. Peel off the papery outside layer and a layer of onion underneath that. For each onion half, cut off the tip of the onion, but leave the root end intact. Cut each onion half in half again from root to tip. Place an onion quarter, flat-side down, on a cutting board. Make several vertical cuts from end to end, being careful not to cut through the root end. Flip the onion quarter onto the other flat side and repeat the vertical cuts, again being careful not to cut through the root end. Then cut the onion crosswise into small, even dice—the pieces should just fall off the knife ready to go. Repeat for each onion quarter.

Continued on next page

3. Press each garlic clove so it gets a little squished, then peel off the papery layer and cut off the root ends (the nubby side). Mince the garlic: Moving the knife blade in a rocking motion, run the knife over the squished cloves repeatedly. Use the knife blade to turn the pile of cut garlic a quarter turn every few seconds. Continue this until the garlic is cut into very fine pieces (minced).

4. Chop the spinach into large pieces.

5. In a large oven-safe skillet, heat the olive oil over medium-high heat.

6. Add the onion and cook for 5 minutes, or until the onion is translucent.

7. Add the garlic and cook for 30 seconds.

8. Stir in the flour and cook for 1 to 2 minutes, or until a paste forms. The paste is called a roux (pronounced as in "kangaroo"), and it is a thickener made when you brown flour and some type of fat (in this case olive oil).

9. Very slowly add the heavy cream and milk, whisking it into the roux constantly to avoid lumps.

10. Reduce the heat to low. Simmer for 8 to 10 minutes, or until the sauce has thickened.

11. Stir in the spinach, parmesan cheese, salt, and pepper.

12. Add the ravioli and stir to combine.

13. Add the mozzarella cheese on top of the ravioli.

14. Transfer the skillet to the oven and bake for 10 minutes, or until the ravioli is heated through. Remove from the oven.

OOPS . . . If you forgot to thaw the ravioli, you can use frozen ravioli. Simply increase the baking time by 10 to 15 minutes.

Per serving: Calories: 611; Total fat: 42g; Cholesterol: 205mg; Sodium: 1824mg; Total carbohydrates: 37g; Fiber: 3g; Sugar: 6g; Protein: 23g

# Veggie Stir-Fry

**Serves 2**
**Prep time: 10 minutes / Cook time: 10 minutes**
VEGETARIAN NO DAIRY NO NUTS FAST

This stir-fry recipe is incredibly versatile. I often use whatever vegetables I have left over in my refrigerator—the only ingredients you really need are the soy sauce, honey, cornstarch, garlic, ginger, and canola oil for the sauce that ties it all together.

**TOOLS AND EQUIPMENT**

Chef's knife

Cutting board

Peeler

Strainer

Small bowl

Measuring cups

Measuring spoons

Rasp grater or fine grater

Whisk

Large skillet

Stirring spoon

**INGREDIENTS**

1 small red onion

2 carrots

6 ounces green beans

8 ounces white mushrooms

1 large garlic clove

¼ cup low-sodium soy sauce

2 tablespoons honey

2 teaspoons cornstarch

1 tablespoon grated fresh ginger

1 tablespoon canola oil

1. To cut the onion into ¼-inch-thick slices, start by cutting the onion in half from root to tip. Peel off the papery outside layer and the layer of onion underneath that. For each onion half, cut off the tip of the onion, but leave the root end intact. Place an onion half, flat-side down, on a cutting board. Cut the onion into ¼-inch-thick slices, so that the layers of the onion come apart into little crescents. Repeat with the other half.

2. Peel the carrots and cut into thin rounds.

3. Trim both ends from the green beans—you can do this using a knife, or you can easily break off the ends of the beans with your fingers.

4. Clean the mushrooms by putting them in a strainer and briefly running them under cold water in the sink, working off any dirt with your hands. Cut the mushrooms into thin slices.

Continued on next page

5. Press the garlic clove so it gets a little squished, then peel off the papery layer and cut off the root end (the nubby side). Mince the garlic: Moving the knife blade in a rocking motion, run the knife over the squished clove repeatedly. Use the knife blade to turn the pile of cut garlic a quarter turn every few seconds. Continue this until the garlic is cut into very fine pieces (minced).

6. To make the sauce, in a small bowl, combine the soy sauce, honey, cornstarch, ginger, and garlic. Whisk until combined, making sure the cornstarch is fully incorporated.

7. In a large skillet, heat the canola oil over medium-high heat until it shimmers.

8. Add the onion and carrots. Cook for 5 minutes, or until the onion has softened.

9. Add the green beans and mushrooms. Cook for 3 minutes.

10. Pour in the sauce and cook, stirring constantly, for about 1 minute, or until the sauce has thickened. Remove from the heat.

Per serving: Calories: 246; Total fat: 8g; Cholesterol: 0mg; Sodium: 1807mg; Total carbohydrates: 41g; Fiber: 6g; Sugar: 27g; Protein: 9g

## Switch It Up

**CHICKEN AND VEGGIE STIR-FRY:** Prepare the sauce as described. Cut 1 boneless, skinless chicken breast into very thin strips. In a large skillet, heat the canola oil over medium-high heat until it shimmers. Add the chicken strips and cook for 3 minutes per side, or until fully cooked. Add the onion and carrots and cook for 5 minutes, or until the onion has softened. Add the green beans and mushrooms and cook for 3 minutes. Pour in the sauce and cook, stirring constantly, for about 1 minute, or until the sauce has thickened.

**STIR-FRY AND NOODLES:** Cook instant ramen noodles according to the package directions, but discard the seasoning packet. Meanwhile, prepare the recipe as described. Once the noodles are cooked, drain and add them to the skillet with the stir-fry. Toss to coat.

# Vegetarian Miso Ramen

**Serves 2**

**Prep time: 10 minutes / Cook time: 20 minutes**

VEGETARIAN  NO DAIRY  NO NUTS  FAST

This recipe uses miso, the salty, protein-rich Japanese fermented soybean paste, and it comes together quickly. It's important that you prep all of the components before you get started.

**TOOLS AND EQUIPMENT**

*Medium saucepan*

*Large bowl*

*Slotted spoon*

*Chef's knife*

*Cutting board*

*Strainer*

*Large saucepan*

*Measuring spoons*

*Rasp grater or fine grater*

*Measuring cups*

*Stirring spoon*

*Ladle*

**INGREDIENTS**

2 large eggs

1 garlic clove

6 ounces baby spinach

6 cremini mushrooms

2 packages instant ramen

½ tablespoon sesame oil

2 teaspoons grated fresh ginger

4 cups vegetable broth

1 tablespoon tamari

2 tablespoons miso

1 scallion

1. Fill a medium saucepan with water, cover with a lid, and bring to a boil over high heat. Fill a large bowl with ice water.

2. Once the water is boiling, using a slotted spoon, carefully place the eggs one at a time into the boiling water. Cook for 6 minutes 30 seconds. Once the eggs have finished cooking, immediately place them in the ice water. Keep the egg water boiling.

3. While the eggs are cooking, press the garlic clove so it gets a little squished, then peel off the papery layer and cut off the root end (the nubby side). Mince the garlic: Moving the knife blade in a rocking motion, run the knife over the squished clove repeatedly. Use the knife blade to turn the pile of cut garlic a quarter turn every few seconds. Continue this until the garlic is cut into very fine pieces (minced).

Continued on page 97

4. Chop the spinach into large pieces.

5. Clean the mushrooms by putting them in a strainer and briefly running them under cold water in the sink, working off any dirt with your hands. Cut the mushrooms into thin slices.

6. Open the packages of instant ramen noodles and discard the seasoning packets.

7. Put the noodles in the saucepan that you cooked the eggs in and cook according to the package directions, usually about 2 minutes, until tender. Remove from the heat. Drain the noodles in a strainer and divide evenly between 2 soup bowls.

8. Meanwhile, in a large saucepan, heat the sesame oil over medium-high heat.

9. Once the sesame oil is hot, add the garlic and ginger. Cook for 30 seconds, or until fragrant.

10. Add the broth, tamari, and mushrooms. Bring to a slight boil. Cook for 2 to 3 minutes. Remove from the heat.

11. Divide the spinach evenly between both bowls of noodles.

12. Stir the miso into the broth until combined.

13. Ladle the broth and vegetables over the noodles.

14. Peel each egg and cut in half. Divide between the bowls.

15. Trim the scallion by cutting off the root end and cutting ½ inch off the top. Cut the remaining onion into little circles. Divide between the bowls.

**DON'T HAVE IT?** If you don't have tamari, you can substitute an equal amount of soy sauce.

Per serving: Calories: 567; Total fat: 24g; Cholesterol: 164mg; Sodium: 3914mg; Total carbohydrates: 68g; Fiber: 6g; Sugar: 9g; Protein: 21g

# Oven-Baked Risotto with Peas

**Serves 4**
**Prep time: 5 minutes / Cook time: 45 minutes**
**NO SOY** NO NUTS

It's important to use Arborio rice for this recipe—you can't make risotto with just any old kind of rice. Named for a town in Italy's Po Valley, Arborio is a shorter grain of rice that's high in starch, which gives risotto its creamy texture.

**TOOLS AND EQUIPMENT**

*Measuring cups*

*Measuring spoons*

*Oven-safe 4-quart stockpot*

*Pot holder*

*Stirring spoon*

*Grater*

*Chef's knife*

......................................

**INGREDIENTS**

5 cups chicken stock, divided

1½ cups Arborio rice

1 cup grated parmesan cheese

1 cup frozen peas

½ cup heavy cream

3 tablespoons unsalted butter, cubed

2 teaspoons table salt

1 teaspoon ground black pepper

1. Preheat the oven to 350°F.
2. Put 4 cups of chicken stock in an oven-safe 4-quart stockpot and bring to a simmer.
3. Add the rice and cover the pot with a lid.
4. Transfer the pot to the oven and bake for 45 minutes, or until most of the liquid has been absorbed and the rice is tender and slightly firm in the center. Remove from the oven.
5. Stir in the remaining 1 cup of chicken stock, the parmesan cheese, peas, heavy cream, butter, salt, and pepper.
6. Stir the rice for 2 minutes, or until the butter has melted and the rice has thickened.

**TRY THIS!** You can make this recipe vegetarian by swapping out the chicken stock for vegetable broth and using vegetarian parmesan.

Per serving: Calories: 583; Total fat: 27g; Cholesterol: 78mg; Sodium: 2313mg; Total carbohydrates: 66g; Fiber: 5g; Sugar: 3g; Protein: 21g

# Cauliflower Parmesan

**Makes 4 or 5 pieces**
**Prep time: 5 minutes / Cook time: 40 minutes**
VEGETARIAN NO GLUTEN **NO SOY** NO NUTS

The American writer and humorist Mark Twain wrote that "cauliflower is nothing but cabbage with a college education," and this recipe adds parmesan to that bachelor's degree. It's important that you leave the stem on the cauliflower when you cut it up, because the stem helps hold the cauliflower pieces together in this dish.

**TOOLS AND EQUIPMENT**

Chef's knife

Cutting board

Strainer

Rimmed baking sheet

Pastry brush

Measuring spoons

Measuring cups

2 small bowls

Stirring spoon

Pot holder

Tongs

Grater

........................................

**INGREDIENTS**

1 large cauliflower

3 tablespoons olive oil

¼ teaspoon table salt

¼ teaspoon garlic powder

¼ teaspoon onion powder

¼ teaspoon ground black pepper

1 cup shredded mozzarella cheese

4 tablespoons grated vegetarian parmesan cheese, divided

¼ cup basil leaves

1½ cups prepared marinara sauce or the marinara sauce on page 86

1. Preheat the oven to 425°F.

2. Peel off any green leaves from the cauliflower. Cut off the dry end of the stem so that you'll have a flat bottom to easily balance the cauliflower on a cutting board. Cut the cauliflower into 1-inch-thick slices. Some of it will fall apart, but you should also have parts that hold together and look like neat little cross-sections of the cauliflower.

3. Rinse the cut cauliflower with cold water over a strainer in the sink, trying to keep the pieces intact. It's inevitable that it'll fall apart a little bit, but do your best.

Continued on next page

4. Arrange the cauliflower on a rimmed baking sheet in a single layer.

5. Brush both sides of the cauliflower with the olive oil.

6. To make the seasoning mixture, in a small bowl, combine the salt, garlic powder, onion powder, and pepper. Mix thoroughly.

7. Sprinkle the seasoning mixture evenly over the cauliflower.

8. Transfer the baking sheet to the oven and roast for 18 minutes.

9. Remove the baking sheet from the oven and flip the pieces over.

10. Return the baking sheet to the oven and roast for 17 minutes. Remove from the oven.

11. While the cauliflower is roasting, in another small bowl, combine the mozzarella cheese and 2 tablespoons of parmesan cheese.

12. Cut the basil into small pieces.

13. Once the cauliflower is done roasting, evenly spread the marinara sauce on it.

14. Evenly sprinkle the shredded mozzarella cheese mixture on top.

15. Switch the oven to broil. The broiler is usually at the top of an oven, so make sure to carefully move the oven rack to the highest position. Return the baking sheet to the oven and broil the cauliflower for 2 to 3 minutes, or until the cheese is bubbly and becomes golden. When you're using the broiler, it's best to stay close and keep watch since food can burn quickly under that intense heat. Remove from the oven.

16. Top the cauliflower with the remaining 2 tablespoons of parmesan cheese and the basil.

TRY THIS! Try swapping out the marinara sauce for prepared pesto. Spread 2 tablespoons prepared pesto on each large piece of cauliflower and top with a slice of fresh tomato and the mozzarella topping in the recipe. Broil and finish with parmesan and basil as the recipe instructs.

Per serving (1 piece): Calories: 320; Total fat: 21g; Cholesterol: 31mg; Sodium: 875mg; Total carbohydrates: 23g; Fiber: 6g; Sugar: 12g; Protein: 14g

# Stuffed Portabella Mushrooms

**Makes 2 mushrooms**
**Prep time: 10 minutes / Cook time: 35 minutes**
VEGETARIAN **NO SOY** NO NUTS

Mushrooms have a lot of water in them—it's almost shocking how much they shrink down as you cook them and the water inside evaporates. With that in mind, it's important that you remove any excess water from the mushrooms before you add the filling.

**TOOLS AND EQUIPMENT**

*Strainer*

*Chef's knife*

*Cutting board*

*Rimmed baking sheet*

*Pot holder*

*Large skillet*

*Measuring spoons*

*Measuring cups*

*Stirring spoon*

*Paper towels*

*Grater*

......................................

**INGREDIENTS**

2 large portabella mushrooms

1 onion

1 cup packed baby spinach

4 cherry tomatoes

1 green bell pepper

2 garlic cloves

2 teaspoons olive oil

1/2 cup seasoned bread crumbs

1/4 cup cream cheese

1/4 teaspoon table salt

1/4 teaspoon ground black pepper

1/2 cup shredded vegetarian mozzarella cheese

1. Preheat the oven to 400°F.

2. Clean the mushrooms by putting them in a strainer and briefly running them under cold water in the sink, working off any dirt with your hands. Cut off the stems and set them aside—they will be used in the filling.

3. Place the mushroom caps, stem-side down, on a rimmed baking sheet.

4. Transfer the baking sheet to the oven and bake for 12 minutes. Remove from the mushrooms from the oven, set them aside to cool for 5 minutes, but leave the oven on.

5. While the mushrooms are baking, chop the mushroom stems into small pieces.

Continued on next page

6. To dice the onion, start by cutting the onion in half from root to tip. Peel off the papery outside layer and the layer of onion underneath that. For each onion half, cut off the tip of the onion, but leave the root end intact. Cut an onion half in half again from root to tip. Place an onion quarter, flat-side down, on a cutting board. Make several vertical cuts from end to end, being careful not to cut through the root end. Flip the onion quarter onto the other flat side and repeat the vertical cuts, again being careful not to cut through the root end. Then cut the onion crosswise into small, even dice—the pieces should just fall off the knife ready to go. Set aside ¼ onion and store any leftover onion.

7. Chop the spinach into large pieces.

8. Chop the tomatoes into small pieces.

9. Cut the pepper into quarters. Remove the stem, white membranes, and seeds from all quarters, then store 3 of the quarters. Cut the remaining quarter into small pieces.

10. Press each garlic clove so it gets a little squished, then peel off the papery layer and cut off the root ends (the nubby side). Mince the garlic: Moving the knife blade in a rocking motion, run the knife over the squished cloves repeatedly. Use the knife blade to turn the pile of cut garlic a quarter turn every few seconds. Continue this until the garlic is cut into very fine pieces (minced).

11. To make the filling, in a large skillet, heat the olive oil over medium-high heat until it shimmers.

12. Add the onion and bell pepper. Cook for 5 minutes, or until soft and translucent.

13. Add the garlic and cook for 30 seconds, or until fragrant.

14. Add the spinach, mushroom stems, and tomatoes. Cook for 3 minutes.

15. Add the bread crumbs, cream cheese (breaking it up into chunks as you add it), salt, and pepper. Cook for 2 minutes, allowing the cream cheese to start melting. Remove from the heat.

16. Using paper towels, carefully remove any excess water that came out of the baked mushrooms.

17. Flip the mushrooms over and divide the filling evenly among them.

18. Top each mushroom with ¼ cup of mozzarella cheese.

19. Return the baking sheet to the oven and bake for 10 minutes, or until the cheese has melted and browned. Remove from the oven.

**THERE'S SOME LEFT:** Reheat leftover mushrooms in a 250°F oven for 5 to 10 minutes. Serve the leftovers on top of your favorite salad greens and dress with a light coating of balsamic vinegar and olive oil.

Per serving (1 mushroom): Calories: 391; Total fat: 24g; Cholesterol: 55mg; Sodium: 1012mg; Total carbohydrates: 32g; Fiber: 4g; Sugar: 8g; Protein: 16g.

# Broccoli-Cheddar Soup

**Serves 6**
**Prep time: 5 minutes / Cook time: 30 minutes**
**VEGETARIAN NO SOY NO NUTS**

Feel free to use some of the broccoli stalks in this soup. Because the dish is blended, you won't even notice them.

**TOOLS AND EQUIPMENT**

*Chef's knife*

*Cutting board*

*Peeler*

*4-quart stockpot*

*Measuring cups*

*Measuring spoons*

*Stirring spoon*

*Ladle*

*Blender*

*Large bowl*

*Grater*

........................................

**INGREDIENTS**

1 onion

2 carrots

4 heads broccoli

8 tablespoons (1 stick) unsalted butter

⅓ cup all-purpose flour

4 cups milk

2 cups half-and-half

Pinch ground nutmeg

1 teaspoon table salt

¼ teaspoon ground black pepper

3 cups grated Cheddar cheese

Vegetable broth, as needed

1. To finely dice the onion, start by cutting the onion in half from root to tip. Peel off the papery outside layer and a layer of onion underneath that. For each onion half, cut off the tip of the onion, but leave the root end intact. Cut each onion half in half again from root to tip. Place an onion quarter, flat-side down, on a cutting board. Make several vertical cuts from end to end, being careful not to cut through the root end. Flip the onion quarter onto the other flat side and repeat the vertical cuts, again being careful not to cut through the root end. Then cut the onion crosswise into small, even dice—the pieces should just fall off the knife ready to go. Repeat for each onion quarter.

2. Peel the carrots and remove both ends. Cut the carrots into small pieces.

3. Remove the stem from the broccoli and trim off the florets.

4. In a 4-quart stockpot, melt the butter over medium heat.

5. Add the onion and carrots. Cook for 5 to 6 minutes, or until softened.

6. Sprinkle the flour on top and cook for 1 minute, or until a paste forms. The paste is called a roux (pronounced as in "kangaroo"), and it is a thickener made when you brown flour and some type of fat (in this case butter).

7. Slowly pour in the milk and half-and-half. Stir until combined.

8. Add the nutmeg, broccoli, salt, and pepper.

9. Reduce the heat to low. Cover the pot with a lid and simmer for 20 minutes, or until the broccoli is tender. Remove from the heat.

10. Ladle the soup into a blender, filling it halfway.

11. Your blender should have a removable part in the center of the lid. Take that removable part out and cover that part of the lid with a kitchen towel as you blend so that steam can escape (if the steam is trapped in the blender, the pressure can build until scalding soup explodes; with the kitchen towel, this won't happen). Pulse the soup in the blender until you get your desired consistency. Pour into a large bowl.

12. Repeat until all of the soup is blended.

13. Pour the soup back into the pot and heat over low heat.

14. Add the Cheddar cheese and stir until completely melted.

15. If the soup is too thick, add vegetable broth to thin it to your liking.

**DON'T HAVE IT?** You can easily make this soup without a blender. Simply cut the broccoli, carrots, and onion into bite-size pieces and prepare as directed. Skip the steps where the soup is blended and enjoy a chunkier version. Though the texture may be different, the soup has the same great flavor.

Per serving: Calories: 612; Total fat: 46g; Cholesterol: 133mg; Sodium: 933mg; Total carbohydrates: 29g; Fiber: 4g; Sugar: 16g; Protein: 25g

# Cheesy Potato Soup

### Serves 6
### Prep time: 10 minutes / Cook time: 40 minutes
**NO SOY  NO NUTS**

It's important that you keep the cut potatoes submerged in a bowl of cold water so they don't turn pinkish or grayish brown. The water prevents the potatoes from oxidizing when the flesh is exposed to air.

**TOOLS AND EQUIPMENT**

*Chef's knife*

*Cutting board*

*Peeler*

*2 large bowls*

*Plate*

*Paper towels*

*4-quart stockpot*

*Slotted spoon*

*Measuring cups*

*Measuring spoons*

*Stirring spoon*

*Strainer*

*Whisk*

*Ladle*

*Blender*

......................

**INGREDIENTS**

6 bacon slices

1 onion

3 garlic cloves

2½ pounds Yukon Gold potatoes

3 tablespoons unsalted butter

⅓ cup all-purpose flour

4 cups chicken stock

2 cups milk

⅔ cup heavy cream

1½ teaspoons table salt

1 teaspoon ground black pepper

⅔ cup sour cream

1. Cut the bacon into 1-inch pieces.

2. Dice the onion by cutting the onion in quarters from root to tip, peeling off the papery outside layers, and cutting off the tip of the onion while leaving the root end intact. Cut each onion quarter into tiny cubes.

3. Press each garlic clove so it gets a little squished, then peel off the papery layer and cut off the root ends (the nubby side). Mince the garlic: Moving the knife blade in a rocking motion, run the knife over the squished clove repeatedly until each clove is cut into very fine pieces (minced).

4. Peel the potatoes and cut into 1-inch pieces. Place in a bowl of cold water.

5. Line a plate with paper towels. Put the bacon pieces in a 4-quart stockpot and cook over medium-high heat for about 5 minutes, until the bacon is crisp and browned. Using a slotted spoon, carefully transfer the cooked bacon to the prepared plate.

6. Add the butter to the bacon fat in the pot, allowing it to melt. Add the onion and cook for about 5 minutes, or until soft and translucent. Add the garlic and cook for 30 seconds, or until fragrant.

7. Add the flour and stir until a paste forms.

8. Drain the potatoes in a strainer and add them to the pot.

9. Slowly whisk in the chicken stock, milk, heavy cream, salt, and pepper until combined.

10. Bring the soup up to a boil and cook for 10 minutes, or until the potatoes are tender and can easily be pierced with a fork. Remove from the heat.

11. Ladle the soup into a blender, filling it halfway.

12. Your blender should have a removable part in the center of the lid. Take that removable part out and cover that part of the lid with a kitchen towel as you blend. Pulse the soup in the blender until you get your desired consistency. Pour into a large bowl. Repeat until all of the soup is blended.

13. Pour the soup back into the pot and heat over low heat. Add the sour cream and cooked bacon pieces. Simmer for 10 minutes. Remove from the heat. Add toppings as desired and serve, like shredded cheddar cheese, chopped chives, and even more sour cream and bacon.

TRY THIS! Try adding other veggies like broccoli, cauliflower or carrots. Cut them into bite-size pieces and add to the soup with the potatoes.

Per serving: Calories: 459; Total fat: 24g; Cholesterol: 72mg; Sodium: 1130mg; Total carbohydrates: 48g; Fiber: 3g; Sugar: 11g; Protein: 14g

California Burger
variation, page 113

# Chapter 5
# Meat and Seafood Meals

Easy Ground Beef
Tacos 110

Cowboy Burgers 112

Grilled Cheese Hot Dogs 114

Chicken Enchilada
Street Fries 116

Oven-Fried Chicken Tenders
with Honey-Mustard Sauce 118

Bacon-Ranch Chicken 120

Parmesan-Crusted
Chicken 122

Steak and Cheese
Quesadillas 124

Cheeseburger Macaroni 126

Beef and Broccoli Stir-Fry 128

Spaghetti Carbonara 130

Honey-Garlic Pork Chops 133

Easy Shrimp Scampi 135

Baked Garlic Butter Cod 138

Crispy Fish Tacos 141

Honey-Glazed Salmon 143

Poke Bowl 145

Turkey Chili 147

Creamy Chicken
Tortellini Soup 149

Lasagna Soup 151

# Easy Ground Beef Tacos

**Makes 4 tacos**
**Prep time: 5 minutes / Cook time: 15 minutes**
**NO SOY  NO NUTS  FAST**

Whether for breakfast, lunch, dinner, or a late-night snack, tacos are always a good idea. The possibilities for toppings and combinations are endless, but some of my favorites are shredded Cheddar cheese, chopped tomatoes, shredded lettuce, sour cream, and guacamole (see the recipe on page 38). Pro Tip: Adding the seasonings to the hot skillet allows the flavors to bloom, giving the tacos a more intense flavor.

**TOOLS AND EQUIPMENT**

*Small bowl*

*Measuring spoons*

*Skillet*

*Stirring spoon*

**INGREDIENTS**

1 teaspoon chili powder

1 teaspoon all-purpose flour

½ teaspoon ground cumin

¼ teaspoon table salt

¼ teaspoon dried oregano

¼ teaspoon garlic powder

¼ teaspoon ground black pepper

⅓ pound ground beef

3 tablespoons canned tomato sauce

1 tablespoon water

4 hard taco shells or 6-inch soft corn tortillas

1. To make the seasoning mixture, put the chili powder, flour, cumin, salt, oregano, garlic powder, and pepper in a small bowl. Stir to combine.

2. Put the ground beef in a skillet over medium-high heat. Using a spoon, break the beef apart.

3. Add the seasoning mixture to the beef and cook for about 5 minutes, or until the beef is no longer pink.

4. Reduce the heat to medium. Stir in the tomato sauce and water. Cook for 7 minutes, stirring occasionally. The sauce will thicken slightly as it cooks. Remove from the heat.

5. Warm the taco shells according to the package directions.

6. Spoon 2 heaping tablespoons of taco meat into each shell and add toppings as desired, such as shredded Cheddar cheese, chopped tomatoes, shredded lettuce, sour cream, and guacamole (page 38).

Per serving (1 taco): Calories: 160; Total fat: 8g; Cholesterol: 33mg; Sodium: 287mg; Total carbohydrates: 10g; Fiber: 1g; Sugar: 1g; Protein: 11g

## Switch It Up

**TURKEY TACOS:** Substitute ⅓ pound ground turkey for the beef. Add 1 tablespoon canola oil to the skillet before browning the turkey.

**SHRIMP TACOS:** Substitute ⅓ pound peeled and deveined shrimp for the beef. Add 1 tablespoon unsalted butter to the skillet before browning the shrimp.

# Cowboy Burgers

**Makes 2 burgers**
**Prep time: 5 minutes / Cook time: 10 minutes**
**NO SOY NO NUTS FAST**

The seasoning mixture for this burger is so versatile, it can be used with any kind of burger you make. When you form the burger patty, use your thumb to make a small indent in the center. This will keep the burger from puffing up when it's cooked.

**TOOLS AND EQUIPMENT**

Grill or skillet

Large bowl

Measuring spoons

Metal spatula

Meat thermometer

Plate

Aluminum foil

.......................................

**INGREDIENTS**

²/₃ pound ground beef

½ teaspoon table salt

½ teaspoon garlic powder

½ teaspoon onion powder

¼ teaspoon ground black pepper

2 Monterey Jack cheese slices

2 tablespoons steak sauce, such as A.1. Steak Sauce

2 hamburger buns

2 tablespoons French fried onions

1. Preheat a grill or skillet to medium heat.
2. Put the beef, salt, garlic powder, onion powder, and pepper in a large bowl. Use your hands to mix until fully combined. Don't overhandle the meat because it can become tough.
3. Form the seasoned beef into 2 patties.
4. Put the patties on the grill and cook for 5 minutes per side, or until the internal temperature of the patties reads 165°F on a meat thermometer.
5. Place 1 cheese slice on each patty.
6. Turn off the heat. Transfer the patties to a plate. Cover with aluminum foil and let rest so the cheese melts a little.
7. Spread 1 tablespoon of steak sauce on the bottom half of each bun.
8. Place the patty on top of the steak sauce.

9. Top each patty with 1 tablespoon of French fried onions and the top bun.

Per serving (1 burger): Calories: 605; Total fat: 31g; Cholesterol: 150mg; Sodium: 1305mg; Total carbohydrates: 29g; Fiber: 1g; Sugar: 7g; Protein: 49g

## Switch It Up

**TROPICAL BURGER:** Prepare the hamburger patties as described through step 4. Once the patties have cooked through, top each patty with a slice of Swiss cheese. Transfer the patties to a plate. Cover with aluminum foil and let rest. Spread 1 tablespoon teriyaki sauce on the bottom half of each bun and top each patty with 1 whole pineapple ring.

**CALIFORNIA BURGER:** Prepare the hamburger patties as described through step 4. Once the patties have cooked through, top each patty with a slice of Cheddar cheese. Transfer the patties to a plate. Cover with aluminum foil and let rest. Put 1 tablespoon ketchup and 1 tablespoon mayonnaise in a small bowl. Stir to combine. Spread 1 tablespoon of the mixture on the bottom half of each bun. Place the patty on top of the sauce. Top each patty with lettuce, tomato, and avocado slices.

# Grilled Cheese Hot Dogs

**Makes 2 sandwiches**
**Prep time: 5 minutes / Cook time: 10 minutes**
NO NUTS  FAST

It may seem odd to use mayonnaise on the outside of the sandwich. However, prepare to have your life changed: Mayo has a high smoke point, which makes it easier to get a crispier exterior on the bread without burning it.

**TOOLS AND EQUIPMENT**

*Chef's knife*

*Cutting board*

*Small bowl*

*Measuring spoons*

*Stirring spoon*

*Large nonstick skillet*

*Tongs*

*Spatula*

**INGREDIENTS**

2 hot dogs

4 scallions

2 tablespoons mayonnaise

¼ teaspoon garlic powder

¼ teaspoon onion powder

1 cup shredded Colby Jack cheese, divided

4 bread slices of choice

1. Cut the hot dogs in half crosswise. Without going all the way through, cut each half down the middle, lengthwise—just cut them enough so that you can open the hot dogs like a book.
2. Trim the scallions by cutting ½ inch off the top and cutting off the root end. Cut the remaining scallions into thin circles.
3. Put the mayonnaise, garlic powder, and onion powder in a small bowl. Stir to combine.
4. Heat a large nonstick skillet over medium-high heat.
5. Put the hot dog halves in the skillet and cook for 2 minutes per side, or until they're slightly browned. Remove from the heat.
6. Divide ½ cup of cheese between 2 bread slices.
7. Place the flattened hot dog halves on top of the cheese.
8. Add the remaining ½ cup of cheese on top of the hot dogs.
9. Divide the scallions between the 2 sandwiches.
10. Place the remaining 2 bread slices on top.
11. Spread half of the mayonnaise mixture on the top of each sandwich.
12. Heat the skillet over medium heat.

13. Once the skillet is hot, carefully place both sandwiches in the skillet, mayonnaise-side down.

14. Spread the remaining mayonnaise mixture on the top of each sandwich.

15. Cook for 2 minutes, or until the bottoms are golden.

16. Flip the sandwiches and cook for 2 more minutes. Remove from the heat.

Per serving (1 sandwich): Calories: 697; Total fat: 44g; Cholesterol: 96mg; Sodium: 1204mg; Total carbohydrates: 50g; Fiber: 11g; Sugar: 13g; Protein: 29g

## Switch It Up

**SPICY NACHO DOG GRILLED CHEESE:** Prepare the hot dogs as described. Assemble the sandwiches by placing 1 slice of pepper Jack cheese on each of 2 bread slices. Place the flattened hot dog halves on top of the cheese. Top each with ¼ cup crushed nacho cheese tortilla chips. Top each with another slice of pepper Jack cheese. Place the remaining bread slices on top. Spread the mayonnaise mixture on the top side of each sandwich. Heat the skillet over medium heat. Once the skillet is hot, carefully place both sandwiches in the skillet, mayonnaise-side down. Spread the remaining mayonnaise mixture on the top sides of each sandwich. Cook for 2 minutes, or until the bottoms are golden, then flip and cook for 2 more minutes.

# Chicken Enchilada Street Fries

**Serves 2**

**Prep time: 5 minutes / Cook time: 20 minutes**

NO GLUTEN  NO NUTS

Ordinarily, "fries" are considered finger food, but you're going to need a knife and fork for this loaded dish. You're welcome.

**TOOLS AND EQUIPMENT**

*Small rimmed baking sheet*

*Aluminum foil*

*Pot holder*

*Measuring cups*

*Can opener*

*2 small bowls*

*Measuring spoons*

*Stirring spoon*

*Strainer*

*Grater*

*Chef's knife*

*Cutting board*

**INGREDIENTS**

2 ounces frozen French fries

1 cup shredded cooked chicken

½ cup canned red enchilada sauce

¼ cup sour cream

2 teaspoons milk

¼ cup canned black beans

¼ cup canned corn

1 red onion

½ cup shredded Cheddar cheese

1 lime wedge

1. Preheat the oven according to the fry package's directions, usually around 425°F. Line a small rimmed baking sheet with aluminum foil.

2. Place the fries on the prepared baking sheet and bake according to the package directions, usually about 20 minutes, or until crispy. Remove from the oven, leaving the oven on.

3. In a small bowl, combine the cooked chicken and enchilada sauce. Put the sour cream and milk in another small bowl. Stir to combine.

4. Drain the black beans and corn in a strainer, then rinse with cold water.

5. To finely dice the onion, start by cutting the onion in half from root to tip. Peel off the papery outside layer and a layer of onion underneath that. For each onion half, cut off the tip of the onion, but leave the root end intact. Cut each onion half in half again from root to tip. Place an onion quarter, flat-side down, on a cutting board. Make several vertical cuts from end to end, being careful not to cut through the root end. Flip the onion quarter onto the other flat side and repeat the vertical cuts, again being careful not to cut through the root end. Then cut the onion crosswise into small, even dice—the pieces should just fall off the knife ready to go. Set aside 2 tablespoons and store any leftover onion.

6. Switch the oven to broil.

7. Top the fries with the chicken mixture and spread the cheese over the chicken.

8. Top with the beans, corn, and onion.

9. Return the baking sheet to the oven and broil for 1 minute, or until the cheese melts. Remove from the oven.

10. Drizzle the sour cream mixture and squeeze the lime wedge over the top of the fries.

**DON'T HAVE IT?** If you don't have cooked chicken, you can substitute canned chicken. Drain the chicken, and using a fork, break it apart before using it.

Per serving: Calories: 393; Total fat: 20g; Cholesterol: 90mg; Sodium: 946mg; Total carbohydrates: 24g; Fiber: 4g; Sugar: 4g; Protein: 28g

# Oven-Fried Chicken Tenders with Honey-Mustard Sauce

**Serves 2**
**Prep time: 10 minutes / Cook time: 20 minutes**
NO NUTS

These crispy chicken tenders are incredibly easy to make and full of flavor. I usually make a double batch because they're great reheated (ideally in a 300°F oven for 5 to 10 minutes).

**TOOLS AND EQUIPMENT**

Wire rack

Rimmed baking sheet

Medium skillet

Measuring cups

Measuring spoons

Shallow bowl

Small bowl

Whisk

Tongs

Meat thermometer

Pot holder

......................................

**INGREDIENTS**

Nonstick cooking spray, for coating the wire rack

1 tablespoon unsalted butter

¾ cup panko bread crumbs

1 large egg

1 tablespoon mayonnaise

1½ tablespoons Dijon mustard

2 tablespoons all-purpose flour

½ teaspoon table salt

¼ teaspoon ground black pepper

½ pound chicken tenderloins

¼ cup honey-mustard dipping sauce

1. Preheat the oven to 400°F. Place a wire rack on a rimmed baking sheet and spray with nonstick cooking spray. If you don't have a wire rack, you can use the wire rack from a toaster oven.

2. In a medium skillet, melt the butter over medium-high heat.

3. Add the bread crumbs and cook for 2 to 3 minutes, or until the bread crumbs turn golden. Remove from the heat. Transfer to a shallow bowl.

4. To make the batter, put the egg, mayonnaise, mustard, flour, salt, and pepper in a small bowl. Whisk until combined.

5. Using tongs, dip the chicken in the batter, ensuring the entire tenderloin is completely coated.

6. Place the tenderloin in the bread crumbs. Using tongs, press the crumbs into the chicken.

7. Place the coated chicken in a single layer on the prepared wire rack.

8. Transfer the baking sheet to the oven and bake for 15 minutes, or until a meat thermometer inserted into the thickest part of the chicken reads 165°F. Remove from the oven.

9. Serve the chicken with the honey-mustard dipping sauce on the side.

**DON'T HAVE IT?** If you don't have (or don't like) honey-mustard for your dipping sauce, you can swap it out for barbecue sauce or ranch dressing.

Per serving: Calories: 448; Total fat: 15g; Cholesterol: 155mg; Sodium: 1469mg; Total carbohydrates: 42g; Fiber: 1g; Sugar: 7g; Protein: 33g

# Bacon-Ranch Chicken

### Serves 2
### Prep time: 5 minutes / Cook time: 25 minutes
NO GLUTEN  NO NUTS

This chicken dish is finished under the broiler. The broiler uses a high level of direct radiant heat, usually from the top of your oven, so whenever you use the broiler, it's a good idea to stay close by and not get distracted—food can burn very quickly when the oven is that hot.

**TOOLS AND EQUIPMENT**

*9-by-9-inch metal baking dish*

*Meat mallet (optional)*

*2 small bowls*

*Measuring cups*

*Measuring spoons*

*Stirring spoon*

*Meat thermometer*

*Pot holder*

*Chef's knife*

*Cutting board*

*Plate*

*Paper towels*

*Skillet*

*Tongs or slotted spoon*

**INGREDIENTS**

Nonstick cooking spray, for coating the baking dish

2 boneless, skinless chicken breasts

½ cup grated parmesan cheese, divided

¼ teaspoon table salt

⅛ teaspoon ground black pepper

¾ cup ranch dressing

¼ cup sour cream

2 bacon slices

1. Preheat the oven to 375°F. Spray a 9-by-9-inch metal baking dish with nonstick cooking spray.

2. If the chicken breasts are thicker than 1 inch, using a meat mallet, pound them so that they're 1 inch thick.

3. Put the chicken breasts in the baking dish.

4. In a small bowl, combine ¼ cup of parmesan cheese, the salt, and pepper.

5. In another small bowl, stir together the ranch dressing and sour cream.

6. Sprinkle the parmesan cheese mixture evenly over the chicken.

7. Slather the ranch dressing mixture evenly over the chicken.

8. Top with the remaining ¼ cup of parmesan cheese.

9. Transfer the baking dish to the oven and bake for 20 minutes, or until a meat thermometer inserted into the thickest part of the chicken reads 155°F. Remove from the oven.

10. While the chicken is baking, cut the bacon into ½-inch pieces.

11. Line a plate with paper towels. In a skillet, cook the bacon over medium-high heat for about 5 minutes, or until crispy and browned. Remove from the heat. Using tongs or a slotted spoon, transfer the bacon to the prepared plate.

12. Once the chicken is out of the oven, switch the oven to broil.

13. Return the baking dish to the oven and broil the chicken for 2 minutes, or until golden and bubbly. Do not walk away because the chicken can burn quickly. The chicken is done when a meat thermometer inserted into the thickest part reads 165°F. Remove from the oven.

14. Top the chicken with the bacon pieces and serve.

**THERE'S SOME LEFT:** Use leftover Bacon-Ranch Chicken as an alternative filling for the Steak and Cheese Hand Pies (page 65).

Per serving: Calories: 718; Total fat: 60g; Cholesterol: 157mg; Sodium: 1840mg; Total carbohydrates: 8g; Fiber: 0g; Sugar: 4g; Protein: 37g

# Parmesan-Crusted Chicken

### Serves 2
### Prep time: 5 minutes / Cook time: 20 minutes
NO NUTS

Parmesan is a hard cheese produced in Italy, named after the region that produces it. The cheese is aged for a year or more! In this recipe, the parmesan crust adds a crispy saltiness to the chicken. You can enjoy this chicken on its own or slice it up for a salad or sandwich.

**TOOLS AND EQUIPMENT**

*Rimmed baking sheet*

*Meat mallet (optional)*

*Measuring cups*

*Measuring spoons*

*Shallow bowl*

*Stirring spoon*

*Pastry brush or butter knife*

*Tongs*

*Meat thermometer*

*Pot holder*

.........................................

**INGREDIENTS**

Nonstick cooking spray, for coating the baking sheet

2 boneless, skinless chicken breasts

1/2 cup seasoned Italian bread crumbs

1/4 cup grated parmesan cheese

1/2 teaspoon garlic powder

1/2 teaspoon onion powder

1/2 teaspoon kosher salt

1/4 teaspoon ground black pepper

1/8 teaspoon ground paprika

2 tablespoons mayonnaise

1. Preheat the oven to 400°F. Spray a rimmed baking sheet with nonstick cooking spray.

2. If the chicken breasts are thicker than 1 inch, using a meat mallet, pound them so that they're 1 inch thick.

3. Put the bread crumbs, parmesan cheese, garlic powder, onion powder, salt, pepper, and paprika in a shallow bowl. Stir to combine until the spices seem evenly distributed.

4. Using a pastry brush, evenly coat each chicken breast with the mayonnaise.

5. One at a time, using tongs, press the chicken breasts into the bread crumb mixture, making sure to coat both sides.

6. Place the chicken on the prepared baking sheet.

7. Transfer the baking sheet to the oven and bake for 15 to 20 minutes, or until a meat thermometer inserted into the thickest part of the chicken reads 165°F. Remove from the oven.

**DON'T HAVE IT?** If you don't have (or don't like) mayonnaise, you can use 2 tablespoons plain yogurt with a dash mustard and a pinch salt and pepper instead.

Per serving: Calories: 401; Total fat: 18g; Cholesterol: 97mg; Sodium: 1283mg; Total carbohydrates: 24g; Fiber: 2g; Sugar: 2g; Protein: 33g

# Steak and Cheese Quesadillas

**Makes 2 quesadillas**
**Prep time: 5 minutes / Cook time: 20 minutes**
**NO SOY  NO NUTS  FAST**

You can often find shaved rib eye or top round beef in the meat department at most grocery stores.

**TOOLS AND EQUIPMENT**

Chef's knife

Cutting board

Large skillet

Measuring spoons

Tongs

Plate

Aluminum foil

2 spatulas

......................................

**INGREDIENTS**

1 onion

1 red bell pepper

1 green bell pepper

1 garlic clove

4 teaspoons olive oil, divided

½ pound shaved beef (rib eye or top round)

¼ teaspoon table salt

⅛ teaspoon ground black pepper

2 burrito-size flour tortillas

3 provolone cheese slices

1. To finely dice the onion, start by cutting the onion in half from root to tip. Peel off the papery outside layer and a layer of onion underneath that. For each onion half, cut off the tip of the onion, but leave the root end intact. Cut an onion half in half again from root to tip. Place an onion quarter, flat-side down, on a cutting board. Make several vertical cuts from end to end, being careful not to cut through the root end. Flip the onion quarter onto the other flat side and repeat the vertical cuts, again being careful not to cut through the root end. Then cut the onion crosswise into small, even dice—the pieces should just fall off the knife ready to go. Repeat with a second quarter and set aside. Store any leftover onion.

2. Cut the red bell pepper in half. Remove the stems, white membranes, and seeds from both halves. Cut 1 half into ¼-inch pieces and store the other half. Repeat with the green bell pepper.

3. Press the garlic clove so it gets a little squished, then peel off the papery layer and cut off the root end (the nubby side). Mince the garlic: Moving the knife blade in a rocking motion, run the knife over the squished clove repeatedly. Use the knife blade to turn the pile of cut garlic a quarter turn every few seconds. Continue this until the garlic is cut into very fine pieces (minced).

4. In a large skillet, heat 2 teaspoons of olive oil over medium-high heat until it shimmers. Add the beef. Season with the salt and pepper. Cook the beef for about 3 minutes, until no longer pink. Transfer to a plate and cover with aluminum foil.

5. In the same skillet, heat 1 teaspoon of olive oil over medium-high heat.

6. Add the red bell pepper, green bell pepper, and onion. Cook for about 5 minutes, or until the peppers have softened and the onion is translucent.

7. Add the garlic and cook for 30 seconds. Return the beef to the skillet and cook until the beef is warmed through. Remove from the heat.

8. Spoon half of the beef filling onto one half of each tortilla, leaving half the tortilla free to fold over.

9. Cut the provolone cheese in half and place 3 halves on top of the beef in each tortilla. Fold each tortilla in half.

10. In the skillet, heat the remaining 1 teaspoon of olive oil over medium-high heat.

11. Place the folded tortillas in the skillet and cook for about 3 minutes until the cheese melts and the outside becomes golden and crispy.

12. Carefully flip the quesadillas over and cook for about 3 minutes, until the other side becomes golden and crispy. The trick to successfully flipping a quesadilla is to sandwich it between 2 spatulas. The extra support helps keep the filling from falling out. Remove from the heat.

Per serving (1 quesadilla): Calories: 581; Total fat: 32g; Cholesterol: 92mg; Sodium: 1009mg; Total carbohydrates: 40g; Fiber: 4g; Sugar: 4g; Protein: 36g

## Switch It Up

**CHICKEN CHEESESTEAK QUESADILLA:** Instead of shaved beef, use ½ pound boneless, skinless chicken breast, finely diced. Prepare the recipe as described.

**LOADED VEGGIE QUESADILLA:** Omit the beef from the recipe. Cook ¼ cup sliced mushrooms, 2 thin tomato slices, and ¼ cup packed baby spinach along with the peppers and onion.

# Cheeseburger Macaroni

**Serves 2**
**Prep time: 5 minutes / Cook time: 15 minutes**
NO SOY NO NUTS FAST

This is one of my teenage son's favorite meals. He often makes a double batch so that he has leftovers for the next day.

**TOOLS AND EQUIPMENT**

*Chef's knife*

*Cutting board*

*Large skillet with high sides and lid*

*Measuring cups*

*Measuring spoons*

*Stirring spoon*

**INGREDIENTS**

1 onion

1 garlic clove

2 teaspoons olive oil

½ pound ground beef

1 teaspoon table salt, divided

¼ teaspoon ground black pepper

2 teaspoons cornstarch

¾ teaspoon garlic powder

1 cup no-sodium beef broth

¾ cup half-and-half

4 ounces rotini

½ cup shredded Colby Jack cheese

1. To finely dice the onion, start by cutting the onion in half from root to tip. Peel off the papery outside layer and a layer of onion underneath that. For each onion half, cut off the tip of the onion, but leave the root end intact. Cut an onion half in half again from root to tip. Place an onion quarter, flat-side down, on a cutting board. Make several vertical cuts from end to end, being careful not to cut through the root end. Flip the onion quarter onto the other flat side and repeat the vertical cuts, again being careful not to cut through the root end. Then cut the onion crosswise into small, even dice—the pieces should just fall off the knife ready to go. Set ¼ onion aside and store any leftover onion.

2. Press the garlic clove so it gets a little squished, then peel off the papery layer and cut off the root end (the nubby side). Mince the garlic: Moving the knife blade in a rocking motion, run the knife over the squished clove repeatedly. Use the knife blade to turn the pile of cut garlic a quarter turn every few seconds. Continue this until the garlic is cut into very fine pieces (minced).

3. In a large skillet with high sides, heat the olive oil over medium-high heat.

4. Add the beef, ½ teaspoon of salt, the pepper, and onion. Using a spoon, break the beef apart. Cook for about 5 minutes, or until the beef is no longer pink.

5. Add the garlic, cornstarch, garlic powder, and remaining ½ teaspoon of salt. Stir to combine.

6. Stir in the beef broth, half-and-half, and pasta until combined. Bring to a simmer and cover the skillet with a lid. Cook for 9 minutes, or until the pasta is tender. Remove from the heat.

7. Add the cheese and stir until combined.

Per serving: Calories: 781; Total fat: 41g; Cholesterol: 158mg; Sodium: 1529mg; Total carbohydrates: 52g; Fiber: 2g; Sugar: 6g; Protein: 48g

## Switch It Up

**ITALIAN CHEESEBURGER MACARONI:** Add 2 teaspoons Italian seasoning when cooking the beef. Replace ½ cup beef broth with ½ cup canned tomato sauce. Prepare the rest of the recipe as described.

**BBQ CHEESEBURGER MACARONI:** Add ¼ cup your favorite barbecue sauce when cooking the beef. Prepare the rest of the recipe as described. Top with 2 crumbled cooked bacon slices.

# Beef and Broccoli Stir-Fry

## Serves 2
### Prep time: 10 minutes / Cook time: 10 minutes

**NO DAIRY  NO NUTS  FAST**

This recipe has a rich, luxurious sauce. It's important that you remove the excess cornstarch from the beef before adding it to the skillet. Cornstarch is a finely ground type of flour; it's used as a thickener in cooking, and if you put too much, it will do its job too well and make the sauce too thick.

**TOOLS AND EQUIPMENT**

*Chef's knife*

*Cutting board*

*Medium saucepan*

*Measuring cups*

*Strainer*

*Zip-top bag*

*Measuring spoons*

*Large skillet*

*Tongs*

*Rasp grater or fine grater*

*Stirring spoon*

**INGREDIENTS**

2 garlic cloves

1 cup broccoli florets

½ pound flank steak

2 tablespoons cornstarch

2 tablespoons canola oil

1 teaspoon grated fresh ginger

¼ cup low-sodium soy sauce

¼ cup water

¼ cup packed dark brown sugar

1. Press each garlic clove so it gets a little squished, then peel off the papery layer and cut off the root ends (the nubby side). Mince the garlic: Moving the knife blade in a rocking motion, run the knife over the squished cloves repeatedly. Use the knife blade to turn the pile of cut garlic a quarter turn every few seconds. Continue this until the garlic is cut into very fine pieces (minced).

2. Fill a medium saucepan with water and bring to a boil over high heat.

3. Once the water is boiling, add the broccoli and cook for 2 minutes. Remove from the heat. Drain the broccoli in a strainer.

4. Cut the steak into ¼-inch-thick slices. Put into a zip-top bag.

5. Add the cornstarch to the bag. Seal the bag, removing any excess air. Shake to coat all the steak in the cornstarch.

6. In a large skillet, heat the canola oil over medium-high heat until it shimmers.

7. Shake off excess cornstarch from the steak, and using tongs, add the coated steak to the skillet in a single layer. Cook for 1 minute per side. Remove the steak from the skillet.

8. Add the garlic and ginger to the skillet and cook for 30 seconds.

9. Add the soy sauce, water, and brown sugar. Bring to a simmer.

10. Add the steak and broccoli. Simmer for 1 to 2 minutes. Remove from the heat.

**TRY THIS!** This recipe is very adaptable. You can add any of your favorite veggies—snow peas, shredded carrots, green beans, and bell peppers would be great.

Per serving: Calories: 464; Total fat: 23g; Cholesterol: 53mg; Sodium: 1229mg; Total carbohydrates: 36g; Fiber: 1g; Sugar: 25g; Protein: 29g

# Spaghetti Carbonara

**Serves 2**
**Prep time: 5 minutes / Cook time: 20 minutes**
**NO SOY** NO NUTS **5 INGREDIENTS OR LESS**

Carbonara is a bacon-and-eggs pasta dish that is simple, rich, and delicious. When you add the parmesan-egg mixture to the pasta, make sure that the skillet is not too hot. You don't want to scramble the egg, just gently warm it through.

**TOOLS AND EQUIPMENT**

*Large pot*

*Heat-safe bowl*

*Measuring cups*

*Measuring spoons*

*Strainer*

*Large skillet*

*Chef's knife*

*Cutting board*

*Small bowl*

*Whisk*

*Grater*

*Stirring spoon*

*Tongs*

**INGREDIENTS**

Salt, for cooking the spaghetti

1 (8-ounce) package spaghetti

2 bacon slices

1 large egg

⅓ cup grated parmesan cheese

2 garlic cloves

½ teaspoon table salt

¼ teaspoon ground black pepper

1. Bring a large pot of salted water to a boil over high heat.
2. Add the spaghetti and cook according to the package directions, usually about 10 minutes, until tender. Remove from the heat. Reserve ½ cup of the cooking water in a heat-safe bowl. Drain the spaghetti in a strainer.
3. Heat a large skillet over medium-high heat.
4. Put the bacon in the skillet and cook for 6 to 8 minutes, or until brown and crispy. Remove from the heat. Reserving 1 tablespoon of bacon fat, transfer the bacon to a cutting board.
5. Chop the bacon into bite-size pieces.
6. In a small bowl, whisk together the egg and parmesan cheese.

7. Press each garlic clove so it gets a little squished, then peel off the papery layer and cut off the root ends (the nubby side). Mince the garlic: Moving the knife blade in a rocking motion, run the knife over the squished cloves repeatedly. Use the knife blade to turn the pile of cut garlic a quarter turn every few seconds. Continue this until the garlic is cut into very fine pieces (minced).

8. Heat the reserved bacon fat in the skillet over medium heat.

9. Once the skillet is hot, add the garlic and cook for 30 seconds.

10. Reduce the heat to low. Add the cooked spaghetti.

11. Stir in the egg mixture, salt, and pepper. Using tongs, gently toss to combine.

12. Slowly stir in reserved pasta water until you get your desired consistency. Remove from the heat.

13. Top the pasta with the bacon pieces before serving.

**SWITCH IT UP:** You can easily use turkey bacon or vegan bacon in this recipe. Cook according to the package's instructions.

Per serving: Calories: 573; Total fat: 12g; Cholesterol: 115mg; Sodium: 1060mg; Total carbohydrates: 89g; Fiber: 4g; Sugar: 3g; Protein: 26g

# Honey-Garlic Pork Chops

**Makes 4 pork chops**
**Prep time: 5 minutes / Cook time: 20 minutes**
**NO DAIRY  NO NUTS**

The key to making this recipe quickly is using thin, boneless pork chops. If you have thicker pork chops, you can cut them through the center so you end up with two thinner ones. Green beans make a great side to this dish.

| TOOLS AND EQUIPMENT | | INGREDIENTS | |
|---|---|---|---|
| Small bowl | Cutting board | ½ cup ketchup | 4 boneless pork chops |
| Measuring cups | Large skillet | 2½ tablespoons honey | ½ teaspoon table salt |
| Measuring spoons | Pastry brush | 2 tablespoons low-sodium soy sauce | ¼ teaspoon ground black pepper |
| Whisk | Tongs | 2 garlic cloves | 1 tablespoon olive oil |
| Chef's knife | Meat thermometer | | |

1. To make the glaze, in a small bowl, whisk together the ketchup, honey, and soy sauce.

2. Press each garlic clove so it gets a little squished, then peel off the papery layer and cut off the root ends (the nubby side). Mince the garlic: Moving the knife blade in a rocking motion, run the knife over the squished cloves repeatedly. Use the knife blade to turn the pile of cut garlic a quarter turn every few seconds. Continue this until the garlic is cut into very fine pieces (minced).

3. Lightly season both sides of the pork chops with the salt and pepper.

4. In a large skillet, heat the olive oil over medium-high heat until it shimmers.

5. Add the pork chops and sear for 7 minutes.

6. Brush or slowly pour some of the glaze over the pork chops.

7. Using tongs, flip the pork chops. Brush some of the glaze on the other side of the pork chops and sear for 5 minutes, or until a meat thermometer inserted into the thickest part reads 145°F.

Continued on next page

8. Pour the remaining glaze into the skillet and simmer for 3 minutes. Remove from the heat.

**THERE'S SOME LEFT:** Thinly slice leftover pork chops and reheat them in a small skillet. Put them in a soft tortilla and top with coleslaw for an easy pork taco.

Per serving (1 pork chop): Calories: 237; Total fat: 8g; Cholesterol: 55mg; Sodium: 1064mg; Total carbohydrates: 20g; Fiber: <1g; Sugar: 17g; Protein: 24g

# Easy Shrimp Scampi

### Serves 2
### Prep time: 5 minutes / Cook time: 20 minutes
**NO SOY  NO NUTS**

Shrimp are some of our most delicious bottom feeders, but be aware that they cook very quickly and turn rubbery when overcooked. Raw shrimp starts off gray and a little translucent, and you will know it's done when the flesh is opaque and the exterior is pinkish.

**TOOLS AND EQUIPMENT**

*Large pot*

*Strainer*

*Chef's knife*

*Cutting board*

*Large skillet*

*Measuring spoons*

*Tongs*

*Bowl*

*Aluminum foil*

*Measuring cups*

*Whisk*

........................................

**INGREDIENTS**

Salt, for cooking the linguine

1 (5-ounce) package linguine

1 onion

1 garlic clove

1 tablespoon unsalted butter, divided

1 tablespoon olive oil, divided

Pinch red pepper flakes

⅓ pound large or extra-large shrimp, peeled and deveined

¼ teaspoon table salt

⅛ teaspoon ground black pepper

¼ cup chicken stock

Juice of ½ lemon

2 tablespoons chopped fresh parsley

1. Bring a large pot of salted water to a boil over high heat.

2. Add the linguine and cook according to the package directions, usually about 10 minutes, until tender. Remove from the heat. Drain in a strainer.

3. To finely dice the onion, start by cutting the onion in half from root to tip. Peel off the papery outside layer and a layer of onion underneath that. For each onion half, cut off the tip of the onion, but leave the root end intact. Cut an onion half in half again from root to tip. Place an onion quarter, flat-side down, on a cutting board. Make several vertical cuts from end to end, being careful not to cut through the root end. Flip the onion quarter

Continued on next page

onto the other flat side and repeat the vertical cuts, again being careful not to cut through the root end. Then cut the onion crosswise into very fine, even dice—the pieces should just fall off the knife ready to go. Set aside ¼ cup and store any leftover onion.

4.  Press the garlic clove so it gets a little squished, then peel off the papery layer and cut off the root end (the nubby side). Mince the garlic: Moving the knife blade in a rocking motion, run the knife over the squished clove repeatedly. Use the knife blade to turn the pile of cut garlic a quarter turn every few seconds. Continue this until the garlic is cut into very fine pieces (minced).

5.  In a large skillet, heat ½ tablespoon of butter and ½ tablespoon of olive oil over medium-high heat until the butter has melted.

6.  Add the onion, garlic, and red pepper flakes. Cook for 3 minutes, or until the onion is softened and translucent.

7.  Season the shrimp with the salt and pepper and add to the skillet. Cook, turning once, for 3 minutes, or until pink. Transfer the shrimp to a bowl and cover with aluminum foil.

8.  Add the chicken stock and lemon juice to the skillet. Bring to a simmer.

9.  Add the remaining ½ tablespoon of butter and ½ tablespoon of olive oil. Whisk until combined and the butter has melted.

10. Add the cooked linguine.

11. Return the shrimp to the skillet, along with any juices that accumulated in the bowl. Using tongs, toss everything together.

12. Top the pasta with the parsley.

Per serving: Calories: 486; Total fat: 15g; Cholesterol: 176mg; Sodium: 929mg; Total carbohydrates: 58g; Fiber: 3g; Sugar: 3g; Protein: 28g

## Switch It Up

**CHICKEN SCAMPI:** Replace the shrimp with ⅓ pound boneless, skinless chicken breast sliced very thinly. Prepare the rest of the recipe as described.

**SCALLOP SCAMPI:** Replace the shrimp with ⅓ pound baby scallops. Prepare the rest of the recipe as described.

**VEGGIE SCAMPI:** Replace the shrimp with 1 cup halved cherry tomatoes and ¼ small zucchini shaved into ribbons using a vegetable peeler. Prepare the rest of the recipe as described.

# Baked Garlic Butter Cod

**Serves 2**
**Prep time: 5 minutes / Cook time: 20 minutes**

NO GLUTEN **NO SOY** NO NUTS

Cod has a mild taste and is both flaky and dense when cooked; it's the perfect canvas for the bold flavor of garlic. Serve this dish alongside the Green Goddess Chopped Salad (page 74).

**TOOLS AND EQUIPMENT**

*9-by-9-inch baking dish*

*Chef's knife*

*Cutting board*

*Small bowl*

*Measuring spoons*

*Stirring spoon*

*Meat thermometer*

*Pot holder*

........................................

**INGREDIENTS**

Nonstick cooking spray, for coating the baking dish

2 garlic cloves

2 tablespoons unsalted butter, at room temperature

1 tablespoon olive oil

⅛ teaspoon paprika

¼ teaspoon table salt

⅛ teaspoon ground black pepper

1 tablespoon finely chopped fresh parsley

2 (4-ounce) cod fillets

1 lemon

1. Preheat the oven to 400°F. Spray a 9-by-9-inch baking dish with nonstick cooking spray.

2. Press each garlic clove so it gets a little squished, then peel off the papery layer and cut off the root ends (the nubby side). Mince the garlic: Moving the knife blade in a rocking motion, run the knife over the squished cloves repeatedly. Use the knife blade to turn the pile of cut garlic a quarter turn every few seconds. Continue this until the garlic is cut into very fine pieces (minced).

3. In a small bowl, using a spoon or even your fingers, combine the butter, olive oil, garlic, paprika, salt, pepper, and parsley. The mixture should resemble a paste.

4. Coat the entire outside of the cod fillets with the butter mixture and place them in a single layer in the prepared baking dish.

5. Cut the lemon into ¼-inch-thick slices. Place 2 slices on top of each piece of cod.

6. Lay the remaining slices around the bottom of the baking dish.

7. Transfer the baking dish to the oven and bake for 20 minutes, or until a meat thermometer inserted into the thickest part of the cod reads 145°F. Remove from the oven.

8. Drizzle the juices from the baking dish over the cod before serving.

**DON'T HAVE IT?** If you don't have fresh garlic, you can substitute ⅛ teaspoon garlic powder.

Per serving: Calories: 259; Total fat: 19g; Cholesterol: 89mg; Sodium: 402mg; Total carbohydrates: 3g; Fiber: 1g; Sugar: 1g; Protein: 21g

# Crispy Fish Tacos

**Makes 4 tacos**
**Prep time: 15 minutes / Cook time: 15 minutes**
**NO SOY NO NUTS**

These tacos have the perfect texture combination—crispy fish, soft tortillas, and creamy coleslaw. If you want to spice things up a little, add some hot sauce to the coleslaw. Some other suggested toppings are sour cream, fresh cilantro, red onions, and guacamole (see recipe on page 38).

**TOOLS AND EQUIPMENT**

*Rimmed baking sheet*

*Aluminum foil*

*Chef's knife*

*Cutting board*

*Medium skillet*

*Measuring cups*

*Measuring spoons*

*2 shallow bowls*

*Stirring spoon*

*Whisk*

*Tongs*

*Meat thermometer*

*Pot holder*

*Fork*

**INGREDIENTS**

Nonstick cooking spray, for coating the baking sheet

½ pound firm white fish, such as cod or halibut

⅓ cup panko bread crumbs

½ teaspoon chili powder

¼ teaspoon garlic powder

¼ teaspoon ground cumin

¼ teaspoon table salt

⅛ teaspoon ground black pepper

1 large egg

4 tortillas, warmed

1 cup premade coleslaw

1. Preheat the oven to 375°F. Line a rimmed baking sheet with aluminum foil and spray with nonstick cooking spray.

2. Cut the fish into 2-inch pieces.

3. Heat a medium skillet over medium-high heat.

4. Once the skillet is hot, put the bread crumbs in the skillet and cook for 2 to 3 minutes, or until golden. Remove from the heat. Transfer to a shallow bowl.

Continued on next page

5.  Add the chili powder, garlic powder, cumin, salt, and pepper. Stir to combine.

6.  In another shallow bowl, whisk the egg.

7.  Set up an assembly line for the coating process—first egg, then bread crumbs, then baking sheet.

8.  Using tongs, dip a piece of fish in the egg, making sure to coat the entire piece.

9.  Next, dip the fish in the bread crumbs, using the tongs to press the crumbs into the fish.

10. Place the coated fish in a single layer on the prepared baking sheet.

11. Repeat until all the fish is coated.

12. Transfer the baking sheet to the oven and bake for 10 minutes, or until a meat thermometer inserted into the center of the thickest part of the fish reads 145°F. Remove from the oven.

13. Using a fork, break the cooked fish into small pieces.

14. Assemble the tacos by placing a layer of coleslaw in each tortilla, followed by the baked fish. Add toppings as desired.

**DON'T HAVE IT?** If you don't have panko bread crumbs, you can substitute an equal amount of cornflakes crushed into fine crumbs. If you're using cornflakes, you do not have to brown them in a skillet.

Per serving (1 taco): Calories: 330; Total fat: 14g; Cholesterol: 76mg; Sodium: 792mg; Total carbohydrates: 34g; Fiber: 1g; Sugar: 2g; Protein: 17g

# Honey-Glazed Salmon

### Serves 2
### Prep time: 5 minutes / Cook time: 10 minutes
NO DAIRY  NO NUTS  FAST

Cooking the salmon skin-side down will help prevent it from overcooking and make the skin extra crispy. Look into which salmon is environmentally responsible to buy, since improper fishery management has had a negative impact on certain populations of salmon.

**TOOLS AND EQUIPMENT**

*Paper towels*

*Chef's knife*

*Cutting board*

*2 small bowls*

*Measuring spoons*

*Whisk*

*Medium skillet*

*2 spatulas*

*Spoon*

......................................

**INGREDIENTS**

2 (6-ounce) salmon fillets

1 lemon

1 garlic clove

1½ tablespoons honey

2 tablespoons low-sodium soy sauce

½ teaspoon red pepper flakes

2 tablespoons olive oil, divided

¼ teaspoon table salt

⅛ teaspoon ground black pepper

1. Using a paper towel, pat the salmon dry—this will help the outside get a little crispier.

2. Cut the lemon in half. Squeeze the juice from 1 half into a small bowl. Cut the remaining half into ¼-inch-thick slices.

3. Press the garlic clove so it gets a little squished, then peel off the papery layer and cut off the root end (the nubby side). Mince the garlic: Moving the knife blade in a rocking motion, run the knife over the squished clove repeatedly. Use the knife blade to turn the pile of cut garlic a quarter turn every few seconds. Continue this until the garlic is cut into very fine pieces (minced).

4. To make the sauce, put the honey, soy sauce, lemon juice, and red pepper flakes in another small bowl. Whisk to combine.

Continued on next page

5. In a medium skillet, heat 1 tablespoon of olive oil over medium-high heat until it shimmers.

6. Season the salmon on both sides with the salt and pepper.

7. Add the salmon, skin-side down. Cook for 3 to 4 minutes, or until the translucent pink flesh becomes opaque all the way up the sides and the skin is crispy.

8. Reduce the heat to low. Carefully flip the salmon over. It may help to use 2 spatulas.

9. Add the remaining 1 tablespoon of olive oil and the garlic. Cook for 30 seconds, or until fragrant.

10. Add the sauce and lemon slices. Cook, spooning the sauce over the salmon as it cooks, for 1 to 2 minutes. Remove from the heat.

**DON'T HAVE IT?** If you don't have honey, you can use the same amount of real maple syrup.

Per serving: Calories: 361; Total fat: 18g; Cholesterol: 95mg; Sodium: 1390mg; Total carbohydrates: 16g; Fiber: 1g; Sugar: 14g; Protein: 34g

# Poke Bowl

### Serves 2
### Prep time: 10 minutes, plus 1 hour to marinate

**NO DAIRY  NO NUTS  NO HEAT NECESSARY**

Poke is a Hawaiian dish of marinated raw fish. Because the concept is similar to sushi, you have to get the freshest sushi-grade tuna you can find. Double-check with the person working at the fish counter to make sure that the tuna you've selected is fresh and sushi-grade.

**TOOLS AND EQUIPMENT**

*Chef's knife*

*Cutting board*

*Measuring spoons*

*Medium bowl*

*Whisk*

*Stirring spoon*

*Small bowl*

*Peeler*

*Box grater*

*Measuring cups*

...............................................

**INGREDIENTS**

½ pound sushi-grade ahi tuna

1 tablespoon low-sodium soy sauce

2 teaspoons sesame oil

2 teaspoons rice vinegar

½ teaspoon honey

2 tablespoons mayonnaise

½ teaspoon sriracha

⅛ teaspoon table salt

Pinch ground black pepper

½ cucumber

½ carrot

2 cups prepared instant rice

¼ cup shelled edamame

1. Cut the tuna into ½-inch pieces.

2. Put the soy sauce, sesame oil, rice vinegar, and honey in a medium bowl. Whisk to combine. (If you're using seasoned rice vinegar, start with ¼ teaspoon of honey and adjust to taste.)

3. Add the tuna to the soy sauce mixture and stir until evenly coated. You can let this marinate in a covered container in the fridge for an hour or more, if you wish.

4. In a small bowl, combine the mayonnaise, sriracha, salt, and pepper.

5. Peel the cucumber and cut into ¼-inch squarish pieces.

Continued on next page

6. Peel the carrot and shred on the large holes of a box grater.

7. Divide the rice, tuna, cucumber, carrot, and edamame between 2 bowls.

8. Drizzle with the sriracha mayo.

**TRY THIS!** This poke bowl is extremely versatile. You can use any of your favorite vegetables—mushrooms, bell peppers, zucchini, avocado, snow peas, etc. You can also use extra-firm tofu instead of fish—just marinate it for at least an hour in the fridge and ideally overnight.

Per serving: Calories: 519; Total fat: 18g; Cholesterol: 56mg; Sodium: 745mg; Total carbohydrates: 52g; Fiber: 3g; Sugar: 3g; Protein: 37g.

# Turkey Chili

**Serves 6**

**Prep time: 5 minutes / Cook time: 30 minutes**

**NO DAIRY  NO GLUTEN  NO SOY  NO NUTS**

If you don't have time to chop whole garlic cloves, you can substitute jarred minced garlic. One teaspoon of minced garlic is equal to about a clove.

**TOOLS AND EQUIPMENT**

*Chef's knife*

*Cutting board*

*4-quart stockpot*

*Measuring spoons*

*Stirring spoon*

*Can opener*

*Strainer*

......................................

**INGREDIENTS**

1 onion

1 bell pepper

3 garlic cloves

1 tablespoon canola oil

2 pounds ground turkey

2 teaspoons table salt, divided

1 teaspoon ground black pepper, divided

1 (16-ounce) can kidney beans

1 (10-ounce) can tomatoes with diced chiles

1 (28-ounce) can crushed tomatoes

2 tablespoons taco seasoning

½ teaspoon dried oregano

1 tablespoon sugar

1. To finely dice the onion, start by cutting the onion in half from root to tip. Peel off the papery outside layer and a layer of onion underneath that. For each onion half, cut off the tip of the onion, but leave the root end intact. Cut each onion half in half again from root to tip. Place an onion quarter, flat-side down, on a cutting board. Make several vertical cuts from end to end, being careful not to cut through the root end. Flip the onion quarter onto the other flat side and repeat the vertical cuts, again being careful not to cut through the root end. Then cut the onion crosswise into small, even dice—the pieces should just fall off the knife ready to go. Repeat for each onion quarter.

2. Cut off the top ⅛ inch of the bell pepper. Then, cut down the sides, removing the pepper flesh from the core and seeds. Cut the pepper into small pieces.

Continued on next page

3. Press each garlic clove so it gets a little squished, then peel off the papery layer and cut off the root ends (the nubby side). Mince the garlic: Moving the knife blade in a rocking motion, run the knife over the squished cloves repeatedly. Use the knife blade to turn the pile of cut garlic a quarter turn every few seconds. Continue this until the garlic is cut into very fine pieces (minced).

4. In a 4-quart stockpot, heat the canola oil over medium-high heat until it shimmers.

5. Add the ground turkey, onion, bell pepper, 1 teaspoon of salt, and ½ teaspoon of pepper. Using a spoon, break the turkey apart. Cook for about 5 minutes, or until the turkey is no longer pink.

6. Add the garlic and cook for 1 minute.

7. Drain the kidney beans in a strainer in the sink.

8. Stir in the tomatoes with diced green chiles, the crushed tomatoes, and kidney beans. Stir to combine.

9. Add the taco seasoning, oregano, sugar, and remaining 1 teaspoon of salt and ½ teaspoon of pepper.

10. Reduce the heat to a simmer. Cook for 20 minutes. Remove from the heat.

**THERE'S SOME LEFT:** Use leftover chili as a topping for chili dogs or chili burgers.

Per serving: Calories: 443; Total fat: 22g; Cholesterol: 118mg; Sodium: 1493mg; Total carbohydrates: 31g; Fiber: 7g; Sugar: 14g; Protein: 33g

# Creamy Chicken Tortellini Soup

**Serves 6**
**Prep time: 10 minutes / Cook time: 35 minutes**
**NO SOY NO NUTS**

This hearty soup is sure to warm you up. If you don't have time to cook the chicken, you can substitute 2 cups of prepared rotisserie chicken.

**TOOLS AND EQUIPMENT**

*Chef's knife*

*Cutting board*

*Peeler*

*4-quart stockpot*

*Measuring cups*

*Measuring spoons*

*Meat thermometer*

*Tongs*

*Plate*

*2 forks*

.....................................

**INGREDIENTS**

1 onion

4 carrots

2 celery stalks

4 garlic cloves

1 tablespoon canola oil

2 teaspoons dried thyme

2 large boneless, skinless chicken breasts

9 cups chicken broth

1 (9-ounce) package tortellini

⅓ cup heavy cream

½ cup packed baby spinach

1 teaspoon table salt

½ teaspoon ground black pepper

1. To finely dice the onion, start by cutting the onion in half from root to tip. Peel off the papery outside layer and a layer of onion underneath that. For each onion half, cut off the tip of the onion, but leave the root end intact. Cut each onion half in half again, from root to tip. Place an onion quarter, flat-side down, on a cutting board. Make several vertical cuts from end to end, being careful not to cut through the root end. Flip the onion quarter onto the other flat side and repeat the vertical cuts, again being careful not to cut through the root end. Then cut the onion crosswise into small, even dice—the pieces should just fall off the knife ready to go. Repeat for each onion quarter.

2. Peel the carrots and cut into ¼-inch pieces.

3. Trim the tops and bottoms off the celery. Cut into ¼-inch pieces.

*Continued on next page*

4. Press each garlic clove so it gets a little squished, then peel off the papery layer and cut off the root ends (the nubby side). Moving the knife blade in a rocking motion, run the knife over the squished cloves repeatedly until the garlic is cut into very fine pieces (minced).

5. In a 4-quart stockpot, heat the canola oil over medium-high heat until it shimmers.

6. Add the onion, carrots, celery, and dried thyme. Cook for 5 minutes, or until softened.

7. Add the garlic and cook for 30 seconds.

8. Add the chicken breasts and chicken broth. Bring to a simmer. Cook for 15 minutes, or until a meat thermometer inserted into the thickest part of the chicken reads 165°F.

9. Using tongs, transfer the chicken to a plate and let cool slightly.

10. Add the tortellini to the pot and stir so it doesn't stick. Cook according to the package directions, usually about 10 minutes, until tender.

11. Meanwhile, using 2 forks, shred the chicken until it reaches your desired size for a bite.

12. Once the tortellini have finished cooking, turn off the heat and return the chicken to the pot.

13. Stir in the heavy cream and add the spinach. Season with the salt and pepper.

Per serving: Calories: 273; Total fat: 10g; Cholesterol: 55mg; Sodium: 2032mg; Total carbohydrates: 29g; Fiber: 3g; Sugar: 6g; Protein: 16g

## Switch It Up

**CREAMY VEGETABLE TORTELLINI SOUP:** Replace the boneless, skinless chicken breast with 1 cup broccoli florets and 1 cup cauliflower florets. Skip the 15-minute simmer time.

# Lasagna Soup

## Serves 2
### Prep time: 5 minutes / Cook time: 30 minutes
**NO SOY  NO NUTS**

This soup has all the flavor of traditional lasagna without the fuss. If the soup gets too thick, you can thin it with a little extra chicken stock.

**TOOLS AND EQUIPMENT**

*Chef's knife*

*Cutting board*

*4-quart stockpot*

*Measuring cups*

*Measuring spoons*

*Stirring spoon*

**INGREDIENTS**

1 onion

1 garlic clove

1 tablespoon olive oil

2/3 pound ground beef

2 teaspoons table salt, divided

1 teaspoon ground black pepper, divided

2 lasagna noodles

2 teaspoons Italian seasoning

1 bay leaf

1 (15-ounce) jar marinara sauce

1 1/3 cups chicken stock

1/4 cup heavy cream

1/4 cup ricotta cheese

1/8 cup shredded mozzarella cheese

1. To finely dice the onion, start by cutting the onion in half from root to tip. Peel off the papery outside layer and a layer of onion underneath that. For each onion half, cut off the tip of the onion, but leave the root end intact. Cut an onion half in half again, from root to tip. Place an onion quarter, flat-side down, on a cutting board. Make several vertical cuts from end to end, being careful not to cut through the root end. Flip the onion quarter onto the other flat side and repeat the vertical cuts, again being careful not to cut through the root end. Then cut the onion crosswise into small, even dice—the pieces should just fall off the knife ready to go. Repeat with 1 more quarter. Store any leftover onion.

Continued on next page

2. Press the garlic clove so it gets a little squished, then peel off the papery layer and cut off the root end (the nubby side). Mince the garlic: Moving the knife blade in a rocking motion, run the knife over the squished clove repeatedly. Use the knife blade to turn the pile of cut garlic a quarter turn every few seconds. Continue this until the garlic is cut into very fine pieces (minced).

3. In a 4-quart stockpot, heat the olive oil over medium-high heat until it shimmers.

4. Add the beef and onion. Season with 1 teaspoon of salt and ½ teaspoon of pepper. Cook for 5 minutes, or until the beef is no longer pink.

5. While the beef is browning, break the lasagna noodles into 1-inch pieces with your hands.

6. Once the beef is no longer pink, drain the excess fat from the pot.

7. Add the garlic, Italian seasoning, bay leaf, marinara sauce, chicken stock, lasagna noodles, and remaining 1 teaspoon of salt and ½ teaspoon of pepper. Stir to combine.

8. Cover the pot with a lid and bring to a boil.

9. Reduce the heat to medium-low and simmer for 20 minutes, or until the noodles are tender. Remove from the heat.

10. Stir in the heavy cream, ricotta cheese, and mozzarella cheese.

TRY THIS! Amp up the flavor of this soup by swapping out half of the ground beef for ⅓ pound ground Italian sausage.

Per serving: Calories: 807; Total fat: 49g; Cholesterol: 187mg; Sodium: 3652mg; Total carbohydrates: 43g; Fiber: 46; Sugar: 20g; Protein: 52g

# Chapter 6
# Desserts

S'more Sundae 157

Perfect Vanilla Cupcakes with Vanilla
Buttercream Frosting 158

Classic Chocolate Cake with
Chocolate Frosting 160

Snickerdoodle Poke Cake 162

Apple-Cinnamon Mug Cake 164

 No-Bake Candy Bar Pie 165

Brownie Pie 167

Chocolate Chip Cookie Bars 169

Potato Chip Cookies 171

Monkey Bread 172

Glazed Donut Holes 175

# S'more Sundae

### Serves 1
### Prep time: 5 minutes / Cook time: 1 minute
NO NUTS  5 INGREDIENTS OR LESS  REALLY FAST

This decadent dessert tastes like a campfire treat. If you don't want to use the broiler to melt the marshmallows, you can toast them over the open flame of a gas stove using metal—not flammable wooden!—skewers.

**TOOLS AND EQUIPMENT**

*Rimmed baking sheet*

*Aluminum foil*

*Zip-top bag*

*Ice cream scoop*

*Pot holder*

**INGREDIENTS**

1 graham cracker

3 scoops fudge swirl ice cream

2 tablespoons chocolate syrup

10 mini marshmallows

1. Set the oven to broil. Line a rimmed baking sheet with aluminum foil.

2. Put the graham cracker in a zip-top bag and crush until the texture resembles fine crumbs.

3. Scoop the ice cream into a bowl, drizzle with chocolate syrup and sprinkle crushed graham crackers on top.

4. Put the mini marshmallows on the prepared baking sheet. Transfer the baking sheet to the oven and broil for 30 second to 1 minute, until the marshmallows start to turn golden. Remove from the oven.

5. Carefully place the marshmallows on top of the sundae and serve.

Per serving: Calories: 609; Total fat: 23g; Cholesterol: 74mg; Sodium: 245mg; Total carbohydrates: 99g; Fiber: 2g; Sugar: 67g; Protein: 8g

## Switch It Up

**STRAWBERRY SUNDAE:** Put 3 scoops strawberry ice cream into a bowl. Put 2 tablespoons strawberry jam in a small microwave-safe bowl. Microwave for 15 to 30 seconds, or until the jam melts. Drizzle the ice cream with the strawberry jam. Top with chopped fresh strawberries, whipped cream, and a cherry.

# Perfect Vanilla Cupcakes with Vanilla Buttercream Frosting

**Makes 24 cupcakes**

**Prep time: 15 minutes / Cook time: 20 minutes, plus time to cool**

**VEGETARIAN NO SOY NO NUTS**

These cupcakes are light, airy, and beautiful. They provide a wonderful blank canvas for all your favorite decorations.

**TOOLS AND EQUIPMENT**

*2 (12-cup) cupcake pans*

*Cupcake liners*

*Large bowl*

*Measuring cups*

*Measuring spoons*

*Stirring spoon*

*2 medium bowls*

*Whisk*

*Electric mixer (handheld or stand)*

*Ice cream scoop or ladle*

*Pot holder*

*Wire rack or plate*

*Spatula*

**INGREDIENTS**

**FOR THE CUPCAKES**

2½ cups all-purpose flour

2 cups sugar

1 tablespoon baking powder

1 teaspoon table salt

1 cup milk

½ cup canola oil

1 tablespoon vanilla extract

2 large eggs

1 cup water

**FOR THE FROSTING**

3 cups powdered sugar

¼ teaspoon table salt

⅓ cup unsalted butter, at room temperature

1½ teaspoons vanilla extract

1 to 2 tablespoons milk

### TO MAKE THE CUPCAKES

1. Preheat the oven to 350°F. Line 2 (12-count) cupcake pans with cupcake liners.

2. In a large bowl, stir together the flour, sugar, baking powder, and salt.

3. Put the milk, canola oil, vanilla, and eggs in a medium bowl. Whisk until completely combined and the mixture is pale yellow.

4. Add the egg mixture to the flour mixture and, using an electric mixer, mix on medium speed.

5. Reduce the mixer speed to low. Slowly pour in the water and mix until combined. The batter will be very thin. Turn off the mixer.

6. Using an ice cream scoop or ladle, fill each cupcake well halfway with the batter.

7. Transfer the cupcake pans to the oven and bake for 15 to 17 minutes, or until a toothpick inserted into the center of a cupcake comes out clean. Remove from the oven.

8. Let the cupcakes cool for 2 minutes in the pans.

9. Remove the cupcakes from the pans and cool on a wire rack or plate. The wire rack is slightly better because there's less warm surface area that touches the bottoms of the cupcakes, but a plate works, too.

### TO MAKE THE FROSTING

10. In a medium bowl, using an electric mixer, mix together the powdered sugar, salt, and butter on low speed.

11. Stir in the vanilla and 1 tablespoon of milk.

12. If needed, gradually mix in the remaining 1 tablespoon of milk until the frosting is smooth and spreadable. Turn off the mixer.

13. When the cupcakes are at room temperature, spread the frosting on them. If the cupcakes are still warm, the frosting will melt.

TRY THIS! You can easily change the color of this frosting by adding food coloring. Start by stirring in just a few drops of your favorite color and add more to adjust as needed.

Per serving (1 cupcake): Calories: 246; Total fat: 8g; Cholesterol: 23mg; Sodium: 195mg; Total carbohydrates: 42g; Fiber: <1g; Sugar: 32g; Protein: 2g

# Classic Chocolate Cake with Chocolate Frosting

### Makes 1 (13-by-9-inch) cake
### Prep time: 15 minutes / Cook time: 30 minutes, plus time to cool

**VEGETARIAN NO SOY NO NUTS**

This is a simple, timeless recipe that I've been making for years. You can change it up by using the vanilla buttercream frosting on page 158.

## TOOLS AND EQUIPMENT

*13-by-9-inch baking dish*

*Large bowl*

*Measuring cups*

*Measuring spoons*

*Stirring spoon*

*Pot holder*

*Medium bowl*

*Electric mixer (handheld or stand)*

*Spatula*

## INGREDIENTS

### FOR THE CAKE

Nonstick cooking spray, for coating the baking dish

3 cups all-purpose flour

2 cups granulated white sugar

⅔ cup cocoa powder

2 teaspoons baking soda

1 teaspoon table salt

2 cups water

⅔ cup unsalted butter, melted

2 teaspoons distilled white vinegar

2 teaspoons vanilla extract

### FOR THE FROSTING

3 cups powdered sugar

⅓ cup unsweetened cocoa powder

⅓ cup unsalted butter, at room temperature

¼ teaspoon table salt

1½ teaspoons vanilla extract

1 to 2 table-spoons milk

## TO MAKE THE CAKE

1. Preheat the oven to 350°F. Spray a 13-by-9-inch baking dish with nonstick cooking spray.

2. Put the flour, sugar, cocoa powder, baking soda, and salt in a large bowl. Stir to combine.

3. Add the water, melted butter, vinegar, and vanilla. Stir until fully combined.

4. Pour the batter into the prepared baking dish.

5. Transfer the baking dish to the oven and bake for 30 minutes, or until a toothpick inserted into the center of the cake comes out clean. Remove from the oven.

6. Let the cake cool completely before frosting.

### TO MAKE THE FROSTING

7. In a medium bowl, using an electric mixer, mix together the powdered sugar, cocoa powder, butter, and salt on low speed.

8. Stir in the vanilla and 1 tablespoon of milk.

9. If needed, gradually mix in the remaining 1 tablespoon of milk until the frosting is smooth and spreadable. Turn off the mixer.

10. When the cake is at room temperature, spread the frosting on it. If the cake is still warm, the frosting will melt.

OOPS . . . If the frosting is too thick, add more milk, ¼ teaspoon at a time. If the frosting is too thin, gradually add small amounts of powdered sugar until it thickens.

Per serving (1 slice): Calories: 514; Total fat: 17g; Cholesterol: 40mg; Sodium: 461mg; Total carbohydrates: 92g; Fiber: 4g; Sugar: 63g; Protein: 5g

# Snickerdoodle Poke Cake

### Makes 1 (13-by-9-inch) cake
### Prep time: 10 minutes / Cook time: 25 minutes, plus 1 hour 10 minutes to cool
**VEGETARIAN**

Poke cakes are one of my favorite desserts to make because they are very forgiving—you bake the cake, then poke holes in it and pour a liquid or syrup on top (in this case, condensed milk), making the cake extra moist and flavorful. Also, it's very soothing to poke holes in a baked good.

**TOOLS AND EQUIPMENT**

13-by-9-inch baking dish

Large bowl

Measuring cups

Measuring spoons

Electric mixer (handheld or stand)

Pot holder

Medium bowl

Whisk

Wooden spoon

Spatula

**INGREDIENTS**

Nonstick cooking spray, for coating the baking dish

1 box yellow cake mix

1 cup water

½ cup canola oil

3 large eggs

1 teaspoon vanilla extract

3 teaspoons ground cinnamon, divided

1½ cups sweetened condensed milk

8 ounces frozen whipped topping, thawed

1. Preheat the oven to 350°F. Spray a 13-by-9-inch baking dish with nonstick cooking spray.

2. In a large bowl, combine the cake mix, water, canola oil, eggs, vanilla, and 1 teaspoon of cinnamon. Using an electric mixer, beat on medium speed until smooth. Turn off the mixer. Pour the mixture into the prepared baking dish.

3. Transfer the baking dish to the oven and bake for 20 to 25 minutes, or until a toothpick inserted into the center of the cake comes out clean. Remove from the oven.

4. Let the cake cool for 10 minutes.

5. Meanwhile, put the condensed milk and 1 teaspoon of cinnamon in a medium bowl. Stir to combine and whisk if the cinnamon clumps up.

6. Using the handle of a skinny wooden spoon, poke holes all over the top of the cake going all the way to the bottom, spacing them about 1 inch apart. If your wooden spoon has a thicker handle, choose a different implement—the holes should be about the circumference of a finger.

7. Pour the condensed milk mixture all over the top of the cake and using a spatula, spread it across the surface, pushing it into the holes.

8. Let the cake cool completely.

9. Spread the whipped topping over the top of the cake, then sprinkle with the remaining 1 teaspoon of cinnamon.

10. Refrigerate the cake for 1 hour before serving.

Per serving (1 slice): Calories: 435; Total fat: 19g; Cholesterol: 54mg; Sodium: 383mg; Total carbohydrates: 62g; Fiber: 1g; Sugar: 42g; Protein: 6g

## Switch It Up

**ORANGE DREAM POKE CAKE:** In a large bowl, combine the cake mix, water, oil, eggs, and 1 teaspoon orange extract. Continue through step 4. In a medium bowl, combine a 3.3-ounce package orange gelatin with 1 cup boiling water and 1 cup cold water. Mix until dissolved. Using a fork, poke holes all over the top of the cake. Spoon the gelatin mixture all over the top of the cake. Continue with steps 8 through 10.

**STRAWBERRY POKE CAKE:** Follow steps 1 through 4 as directed. In a medium bowl, combine a 3.3-ounce package strawberry gelatin with 1 cup boiling water and 1 cup cold water. Mix until dissolved. Using a fork, poke holes all over the top of the cake. Spoon the gelatin mixture all over the top of the cake. Continue with steps 8 through 10.

# Apple-Cinnamon Mug Cake

### Makes 1 mug cake
### Prep time: 5 minutes / Cook time: 1 minute
**VEGETARIAN NO SOY NO NUTS REALLY FAST**

This is a great recipe when you're craving something sweet but also want to spend minimal time in the kitchen. You also have minimal cleanup time, since the only things that need washing are a spoon, some measuring spoons, and a humble mug.

**TOOLS AND EQUIPMENT**

*Microwave-safe mug*

*Measuring spoons*

*Stirring spoon*

**INGREDIENTS**

3 tablespoons all-purpose flour

1 heaping tablespoon light brown sugar

½ teaspoon ground cinnamon

⅛ teaspoon baking powder

1 tablespoon applesauce

½ tablespoon canola oil

½ tablespoon milk

⅛ teaspoon vanilla extract

1. In a small, microwave-safe mug, stir together the flour, brown sugar, cinnamon, and baking powder.

2. Add the applesauce and mix until just combined (it will be thick and sticky).

3. Add the canola oil, milk, and vanilla. Stir until wet, being careful to not overmix.

4. Microwave on high for about 45 seconds, or until the top of the cake is firm. Cooking times may vary depending on microwave strength. If more time is needed, add 10 seconds at a time, checking in between.

OOPS . . . If you start adding the ingredients and realize your mug is too small, transfer the ingredients to a bowl, and prepare the recipe as described. Before cooking the cake, divide the batter evenly between 2 mugs. Microwave each mug separately.

Per serving (1 cake): Calories: 199; Total fat: 7g; Cholesterol: <1mg; Sodium: 68mg; Total carbohydrates: 31g; Fiber: 2g; Sugar: 12g; Protein: 3g

# No-Bake Candy Bar Pie

**Serves 8**

**Prep time: 15 minutes, plus 4 hours to chill**

VEGETARIAN NO HEAT NECESSARY

This pie always gets rave reviews, and it only takes minutes to make. The hardest part is waiting until it sets up before digging in.

**TOOLS AND EQUIPMENT**

Chef's knife

Cutting board

Large bowl

Stirring spoon

Rubber spatula

Measuring cups

**INGREDIENTS**

10 fun-size Snickers bars

16 ounces frozen whipped topping, thawed

1 (14-ounce) jar caramel sauce

1 prepared graham cracker pie crust

½ cup chopped peanuts

Chocolate syrup, for topping

1. Chop the Snickers bars into small pieces.
2. Put the whipped topping in a large bowl.
3. Gently stir in the caramel sauce.
4. Fold in all but ¼ cup chopped Snickers bars. Pour the mixture into the crust.
5. Sprinkle the reserved chopped Snickers on top.
6. Sprinkle the peanuts on top.
7. Drizzle with chocolate syrup.
8. Refrigerate the pie for 4 hours before serving.

Per serving: Calories: 521; Total fat: 26g; Cholesterol: 2mg; Sodium: 338mg; Total carbohydrates: 72g; Fiber: 3g; Sugar: 39g; Protein: 7g

Continued on next page

## Switch It Up

**NO-BAKE BUTTERFINGER PIE:** Chop 10 fun-size Butterfinger candy bars into small pieces. In a large bowl, combine all but ¼ cup chopped Butterfingers, 8 ounces room-temperature cream cheese, and 12 ounces whipped topping. Pour the mixture into a graham cracker pie crust. Sprinkle the reserved ¼ cup chopped Butterfingers on top. Refrigerate for 4 hours before serving.

**NO-BAKE TWIX PIE:** Chop 10 fun-size Twix candy bars into small pieces. In a large bowl, combine 16 ounces whipped topping with 14 ounces caramel sauce. Fold in all but ¼ cup chopped Twix candy bars. Pour the mixture into a graham cracker pie crust. Sprinkle the reserved ¼ cup chopped Twix candy bars on top. Refrigerate for 4 hours before serving.

**NO-BAKE OREO PIE:** Chop 10 Oreo cookies into small pieces. In a large bowl, combine all but ¼ cup chopped Oreos with 8 ounces room-temperature cream cheese and 12 ounces whipped topping. Pour the mixture into an Oreo cookie pie crust. Sprinkle the reserved ¼ cup chopped Oreos on top. Refrigerate for 4 hours before serving.

# Brownie Pie

**Makes 1 pie**
**Prep time: 25 minutes / Cook time: 30 minutes**
VEGETARIAN **NO SOY** NO NUTS

The secret to tender brownies is not overmixing the batter. When you mix flour with wet ingredients, gluten proteins that give necessary structure to any flour-based baked good are activated, but overmixing can overactivate these proteins, making the end product too tough. Stir the ingredients in until they are just combined to avoid overmixing.

**TOOLS AND EQUIPMENT**

*Large pie plate*

*Large bowl*

*Measuring cups*

*Measuring spoons*

*Whisk*

*Medium bowl*

*Stirring spoon*

*Pot holder*

......................................

**INGREDIENTS**

Nonstick cooking spray, for coating the pie plate

1 cup (2 sticks) unsalted butter, melted

1 cup granulated white sugar

1 cup packed light brown sugar

4 large eggs, at room temperature

2 teaspoons vanilla extract

1 cup all-purpose flour

1 cup unsweetened cocoa powder

1 teaspoon table salt

1 cup chocolate chips

1. Preheat the oven to 350°F. Spray a large pie plate with nonstick cooking spray.
2. Put the butter, granulated sugar, and brown sugar in a large bowl. Whisk to combine.
3. Whisk in the eggs one at a time, completely incorporating each egg into the batter before adding the next.
4. Whisk in the vanilla.
5. Put the flour, cocoa powder, and salt in a medium bowl. Whisk to combine.

Continued on next page

6. Add the flour mixture to the egg mixture. Stir gently until just combined. Do not overmix the batter. Pour into the prepared pie plate.

7. Transfer the pie plate to the oven and bake for 30 minutes, or until the brownie pie is set to the touch of a spoon. It may still be soft in the center. Remove from the oven.

8. Let the pie cool. As it cools, it will continue to set up.

**TRY THIS!** Get nutty. Try adding ½ cup of your favorite nuts to the recipe.

Per serving: Calories: 614; Total fat: 34g; Cholesterol: 160mg; Sodium: 355mg; Total carbohydrates: 75g; Fiber: 5g; Sugar: 55g; Protein: 9g

# Chocolate Chip Cookie Bars

**Makes 24 bars**
**Prep time: 10 minutes / Cook time: 25 minutes**
VEGETARIAN **NO SOY** NO NUTS

If you like chocolate chip cookies, you will love these cookie bars. They are delicious on their own, or you can top them with a scoop of ice cream and a drizzle of chocolate syrup.

**TOOLS AND EQUIPMENT**

*13-by-9-inch baking dish*

*2 large bowls*

*Measuring cups*

*Measuring spoons*

*Spatula*

*Whisk*

*Pot holder*

.................................

**INGREDIENTS**

Nonstick cooking spray, for coating the baking dish

2¼ cups all-purpose flour

1 teaspoon baking soda

1 teaspoon table salt

1 cup (2 sticks) unsalted butter, at room temperature

¾ cup granulated white sugar

¾ cup packed light brown sugar

1 teaspoon vanilla extract

2 large eggs

2 cups semisweet chocolate chips

1. Preheat the oven to 375°F. Spray a 13-by-9-inch baking dish with nonstick cooking spray.

2. Put the flour, baking soda, and salt in a large bowl. Using a spatula, stir to combine.

3. Put the butter, granulated sugar, brown sugar, vanilla, and 1 egg in another large bowl. Whisk until combined. Add the remaining egg, whisking until fully combined.

4. To make the batter, add the flour mixture 1 cup at a time, stirring after each addition, to the egg mixture.

5. Add the chocolate chips and stir until just combined. Be careful not to overmix, because overmixing flour with wet ingredients creates a tougher texture than you want.

6. Transfer the batter to the prepared baking dish and, using a spatula, press it into the dish.

**Continued on next page**

7. Transfer the baking dish to the oven and bake for 20 to 25 minutes, or until the bars are golden. Remove from the oven.

8. Let the bars cool completely before cutting into 24 bars.

OOPS . . . Forgot to soften the butter? No problem. Fill a tall drinking glass three-fourths full of warm tap water. Place the stick of butter (still in its wrapper) in the glass. After a few minutes, the butter will be softened.

Per serving (1 bar): Calories: 241; Total fat: 13g; Cholesterol: 36mg; Sodium: 161mg; Total carbohydrates: 32g; Fiber: 1g; Sugar: 21g; Protein: 3g

# Potato Chip Cookies

**Makes 24 cookies**
**Prep time: 10 minutes / Cook time: 15 minutes**
VEGETARIAN  NO SOY  NO NUTS  5 INGREDIENTS OR LESS

This recipe may seem a little wacky, but these cookies are delicious! Potato chips and cookies come together here and form a junk food power couple. The chips add a great texture and a slight saltiness to the cookies.

**TOOLS AND EQUIPMENT**

*Large bowl*

*Measuring cups*

*Measuring spoons*

*Electric mixer (handheld or stand)*

*Spatula*

*Teaspoon*

*Rimmed baking sheet*

*Pot holder*

.................................

**INGREDIENTS**

2 cups (4 sticks) unsalted butter, at room temperature

1 cup sugar

2 teaspoons vanilla extract

3½ cups all-purpose flour

1 cup crushed potato chips

1. Preheat the oven to 350°F.

2. In a large bowl, using an electric mixer, mix together the butter, sugar, and vanilla on medium speed until fully combined.

3. Reduce the mixer speed to low. Slowly add the flour and mix until just combined. Turn off the mixer.

4. Using a spatula, fold in the potato chips. Folding means to gently mix something with a delicate texture—in this case, the chips—into something with a heavier texture—in this case, the cookie bar dough.

5. Drop teaspoonfuls of the dough at least 1 inch apart on a rimmed baking sheet.

6. Transfer the baking sheet to the oven and bake for 15 minutes, or until lightly browned on bottom.

**TRY THIS!** Try experimenting with different flavors. Swap out the vanilla extract for almond extract or orange extract.

Per serving (1 cookie): Calories: 248; Total fat: 16g; Cholesterol: 41mg; Sodium: 15mg; Total carbohydrates: 24g; Fiber: 1g; Sugar: 9g; Protein: 2g

# Monkey Bread

**Makes 1 pull-apart cake**
**Prep time: 15 minutes / Cook time: 35 minutes**

VEGETARIAN  NO NUTS  5 INGREDIENTS OR LESS

This is one of the first recipes my brother learned to cook when he was young. A monkey wouldn't use a knife or fork to eat baked goods, and you don't need a knife or fork to eat this, either—simply pull the pieces apart with your fingers.

**TOOLS AND EQUIPMENT**

*9- or 10-inch Bundt pan*

*Chef's knife*

*Cutting board*

*Measuring cups*

*Measuring spoons*

*Large zip-top bag*

*Small saucepan*

*Rubber spatula*

*Pot holder*

*Plate*

**INGREDIENTS**

Nonstick cooking spray, for coating the pan

3 (12-ounce) packages refrigerated biscuit dough (do not use the flaky layers variety)

1 cup granulated white sugar

2 teaspoons ground cinnamon

8 tablespoons (1 stick) unsalted butter

1 cup packed light brown sugar

1. Preheat the oven to 350°F. Spray a 9- or 10-inch Bundt pan with nonstick cooking spray.

2. Cut each biscuit into quarters.

3. Put the granulated sugar and cinnamon in a large zip-top bag.

4. Add 8 biscuit pieces to the bag and shake until the biscuits are completely coated.

5. Arrange the coated biscuit pieces in the prepared pan. The pieces will puff up and stick together when baked.

6. Repeat steps 4 and 5 with the remaining biscuits.

7. In a small saucepan, melt the butter and brown sugar over medium heat. Bring to a boil and cook for 1 minute. Remove from the heat. Pour over the biscuits.

8. Transfer the Bundt pan to the oven and bake for 35 minutes. Remove from the oven.

9. Let the bread cool in the pan for 10 minutes.

10. Place a large plate on top of the pan.

11. Holding the plate tightly against the pan, flip the pan over, and gently shake or tap the pan to release the monkey bread.

**TRY THIS!** Add ½ cup raisins or ½ cup chopped walnuts or pecans. Spread the raisins or nuts among the biscuit pieces as you add them to the pan.

Per serving (1 slice): Calories: 452; Total fat: 17g; Cholesterol: 20mg; Sodium: 913mg; Total carbohydrates: 71g; Fiber: 2g; Sugar: 38g; Protein: 5g

# Glazed Donut Holes

**Makes 32 donut holes**
**Prep time: 10 minutes / Cook time: 10 minutes**
VEGETARIAN NO NUTS **5 INGREDIENTS OR LESS FAST**

The next time you get a donut craving, whip up a batch of these gems. You can even get creative and try different fillings and glazes.

**TOOLS AND EQUIPMENT**

4-quart stockpot

Heat-safe plate

Paper towels

Meat or candy thermometer

Chef's knife

Cutting board

Tongs

Rimmed baking sheet

Wax paper

Medium bowl

Measuring cups

Whisk

............................

**INGREDIENTS**

Canola oil

1 (12-ounce) package refrigerated biscuit dough (do not use the flaky layers variety)

1 cup powdered sugar

¼ cup milk

1. Fill a 4-quart stockpot with 1½ inches of canola oil. Line a heat-safe plate with paper towels. Heat the oil to 350°F over medium heat. Using a meat or candy thermometer, test the oil to make sure it is at the proper temperature.

2. Separate each biscuit and cut each biscuit into quarters. Roll them into balls.

3. Working in batches of 4 or 5 balls at time, carefully add them to the hot oil with tongs.

4. Cook for about 5 minutes, until the donut holes start to brown on the bottom. Use tongs to carefully flip the donut holes over.

5. Cook the donut holes on the other side for about 5 minutes, or until evenly browned, then remove them from the oil and place on the prepared plate.

6. Line a rimmed baking sheet with wax paper.

Continued on next page

7. To make the glaze, in a medium bowl, whisk together the powdered sugar and milk until completely combined.

8. Dip the donut holes into the glaze and using tongs, make sure they are completely covered.

9. Let the glazed donut holes dry on the prepared baking sheet.

**TRY THIS!** Instead of coating the donut holes in the glaze, mix ½ cup sugar with ½ teaspoon ground cinnamon in a small bowl. Roll the donut holes in the cinnamon-sugar mixture until they are completely covered.

Per serving (1 donut hole): Calories: 47; Total fat: 1g; Cholesterol: <1mg; Sodium: 114mg; Total carbohydrates: 8g; Fiber: <1g; Sugar: 4g; Protein: 1g

# Cooking Terms You Should Know

## A GLOSSARY OF COMMON TERMS

**Boil:** Cooking in bubbling water that has reached 212°F.

**Chop:** Cutting into bite-size or smaller pieces roughly the same size.

**Consistency:** The thickness or texture of an ingredient, sauce, or dish.

**Crosswise:** Slicing horizontally across an ingredient.

**Dash:** A small amount of a liquid ingredient that is roughly equivalent to 1/8 teaspoon.

**Dice:** Cutting food into very small cubes, usually 1/8 to 1/4 inch.

**Divided:** Separating an ingredient that is used in more than one step.

**Dredge:** Coating food in bread crumbs, flour, or another dry ingredient.

**Lengthwise:** Slicing vertically along an ingredient.

**Mash:** Applying pressure using a tool, such as a fork, to break down an ingredient.

**Mince:** Cutting into very tiny pieces.

**Pinch:** A small amount of a dry ingredient—usually herbs, spices, or seasonings—that is roughly equivalent to 1/16 teaspoon.

**Preheat:** Turning on an oven or applying heat to a pan or pot and bringing it up to temperature.

**Rest:** Allowing food to sit, undisturbed, for a period of time.

**Room temperature:** Softening an ingredient, such as butter, by allowing it to sit out until it is about 70°F.

**Serrated:** A blade with teeth or notches.

**Shred:** Rubbing foods against a serrated surface or fork to produce shredded or fine bits.

**Simmer:** Cooking in hot liquid that is just below the boiling point. Bubbles form around the edges, with tiny bubbles that may break through the surface of the liquid.

**Stand:** Allowing food to sit or cool at room temperature for a period of time.

**Substitute:** Replacing one ingredient with another.

**Transfer:** To move food from one vessel to another, such as from a pan to a plate, or from one heat source to another, such as from the stove to the oven.

**Whisk:** Using a fork or whisk to quickly beat ingredients to mix them and incorporate air.

# MEASUREMENT CONVERSIONS

| Volume Equivalents | U.S. Standard | U.S. Standard (ounces) | Metric (approximate) |
|---|---|---|---|
| **Liquid** | 2 tablespoons | 1 fl. oz. | 30 mL |
| | ¼ cup | 2 fl. oz. | 60 mL |
| | ½ cup | 4 fl. oz. | 120 mL |
| | 1 cup | 8 fl. oz. | 240 mL |
| | 1½ cups | 12 fl. oz. | 355 mL |
| | 2 cups or 1 pint | 16 fl. oz. | 475 mL |
| | 4 cups or 1 quart | 32 fl. oz. | 1 L |
| | 1 gallon | 128 fl. oz. | 4 L |
| **Dry** | ⅛ teaspoon | — | 0.5 mL |
| | ¼ teaspoon | — | 1 mL |
| | ½ teaspoon | — | 2 mL |
| | ¾ teaspoon | — | 4 mL |
| | 1 teaspoon | — | 5 mL |
| | 1 tablespoon | — | 15 mL |
| | ¼ cup | — | 59 mL |
| | ⅓ cup | — | 79 mL |
| | ½ cup | — | 118 mL |
| | ⅔ cup | — | 156 mL |
| | ¾ cup | — | 177 mL |
| | 1 cup | — | 235 mL |
| | 2 cups or 1 pint | — | 475 mL |
| | 3 cups | — | 700 mL |
| | 4 cups or 1 quart | — | 1 L |
| | ½ gallon | — | 2 L |
| | 1 gallon | — | 4 L |

## Oven Temperatures

| Fahrenheit | Celsius (approximate) |
|---|---|
| 250°F | 120°C |
| 300°F | 150°C |
| 325°F | 165°C |
| 350°F | 180°C |
| 375°F | 190°C |
| 400°F | 200°C |
| 425°F | 220°C |
| 450°F | 230°C |

## Weight Equivalents

| U.S. Standard | Metric (approximate) |
|---|---|
| ½ ounce | 15 g |
| 1 ounce | 30 g |
| 2 ounces | 60 g |
| 4 ounces | 115 g |
| 8 ounces | 225 g |
| 12 ounces | 340 g |
| 16 ounces or 1 pound | 455 g |

# Resources

**AmericasTestKitchen.com:** for cooking resources and trusted recipes

**BudgetBytes.com:** for recipes that are budget-friendly

**Epicurious.com:** for recipes, cook tips, and videos

**ItIsAKeeper.com:** for easy recipes using easy-to-find ingredients

**TheKitchn.com:** for recipes, tips, and celebrity features

**LoveFoodHateWaste.com:** for inspiration and recipes using leftover ingredients

**USDA.gov:** for comprehensive nutrition and food safety resources

# Recipe Labels Index

## Fast (20 minutes or less)

Apple, Walnut, and Cranberry
    Salad, 72–73
Banana-Walnut Breakfast Couscous, 29
BBQ Cheeseburger Macaroni, 127
Beef and Broccoli Stir-Fry, 128–129
Blueberry Breakfast Couscous, 29
California Burger, 113
Cheeseburger Macaroni, 126–127
Chicken Cheesesteak Quesadilla, 125
Cinnamon-Raisin Breakfast
    Couscous, 28–29
Cinnamon-Sugar Potato Chips, 50
Classic Turkey Club Sandwiches, 61–62
Cowboy Burgers, 112–113
Easy Ground Beef Tacos, 110–111
Everything Bagel Potato Chips, 50
Garlic and Onion Potato Chips, 50
Glazed Donut Holes, 175–176
Grilled Cheese Hot Dogs, 114–115
Hard- and Soft-Boiled Eggs, 21
Honey-Glazed Salmon, 143–144
Italian Cheeseburger Macaroni, 127
Loaded Sheet Pan Nachos, 40–41
Loaded Veggie Quesadilla, 125
Microwave Potato Chips, 49–50
Perfect Omelet, The, 19–20
Roast Beef Club Sandwich, 62
Shrimp Tacos, 111
Spicy Nacho Dog Grilled Cheese, 115
Steak and Cheese Quesadillas, 124–125
Strawberry Cheesecake
    Grilled Cheese, 34
Strawberry-Pecan Breakfast
    Couscous, 29
Tropical Burgers, 113
Turkey Tacos, 111
Vegetarian Miso Ramen, 95–97
Veggie Stir-Fry, 93–94

## 5 ingredients or less

Cheesy Microwave Scramble, 16–17
Cinnamon-Sugar Potato Chips, 50
Everything Bagel Avocado Toast, 22–23
Everything Bagel Potato Chips, 50
Garlic and Onion Potato Chips, 50
Glazed Donut Holes, 175–176
Hard- and Soft-Boiled Eggs, 21
Matcha-Pineapple Smoothie, 33
Microwave Potato Chips, 49–50
Monkey Bread, 172–173
Peanut Butter and Banana Panini, 58–59
Perfect Omelet, The, 19–20
Potato Chip Cookies, 171
S'more Sundae, 157
Soft-Boiled Egg Avocado Toast, 23
Spaghetti Carbonara, 130–131
Strawberry Cheesecake
    Grilled Cheese, 34
Strawberry Sundae, 157

## No dairy

Beef and Broccoli Stir-Fry, 128–129
Blueberry Overnight Oats, 27
Chicken and Veggie Stir-Fry, 94
Choose Your Own Frozen Fruit
    Adventure Overnight Oats, 27
Cinnamon-Sugar Potato Chips, 50
Classic Guacamole, 38–39
Classic Turkey Club Sandwiches, 61–62
Everything Bagel Avocado Toast, 22–23
Everything Bagel Potato Chips, 50
Fruit Salad with Honey-Citrus
    Dressing, 78–79
Fruit Salad with Mint Dressing, 79
Garlic and Onion Potato Chips, 50
Hard- and Soft-Boiled Eggs, 21
Honey-Garlic Pork Chops, 133–134
Honey-Glazed Salmon, 143–144
Maple Granola with Cranberries, 51–53
Mediterranean Chickpea Salad, 82–83
Melon Salad, 79
Microwave Potato Chips, 49–50
Peanut Butter Overnight Oats, 27
Poke Bowl, 145–146
Snickerdoodle Overnight Oats, 26–27
Soft-Boiled Egg Avocado Toast, 23
Stir-Fry and Noodles, 94
Strawberry-Almond Overnight Oats, 27
Tropical Fruit Salad, 79
Turkey Chili, 147–148
Vegetarian Miso Ramen, 95–97
Veggie Stir-Fry, 93–94

## No gluten

Apple-Cinnamon Baked Oatmeal, 24–25
Apple, Walnut, and Cranberry
    Salad, 72–73
Bacon and Cheese Tater Tot
    Kebabs, 42–43
Bacon-Ranch Chicken, 120–121
Baked Garlic Butter Cod, 138–139
Blueberry-Banana Smoothie Bowl, 31–32
Blueberry Overnight Oats, 27
Cauliflower Parmesan, 99–100

Cheesy Microwave Scramble, 16–17
Chicken Enchilada Street Fries, 116–117
Chocolate, Peanut Butter, and
    Banana Smoothie Bowl, 32
Choose Your Own Frozen Fruit
    Adventure Overnight Oats, 27
Cinnamon-Sugar Potato Chips, 50
Classic Guacamole, 38–39
Deconstructed Spicy-Tangy
    Elote Salad, 76–77
Everything Bagel Potato Chips, 50
Fruit Salad with Honey-Citrus
    Dressing, 78–79
Fruit Salad with Mint Dressing, 79
Garlic and Onion Potato Chips, 50
Green Goddess Chopped Salad, 74–75
Hard- and Soft-Boiled Eggs, 21
Loaded Sheet Pan Nachos, 40–41
Maple Granola with Cranberries, 51–53
Matcha-Pineapple Smoothie, 33
Mediterranean Chickpea Salad, 82–83
Melon Salad, 79
Microwave Potato Chips, 49–50
Peanut Butter Overnight Oats, 27
Perfect Omelet, The, 19–20
Pizza Omelet, 20
Snickerdoodle Overnight Oats, 26–27
Southwest Quinoa Salad, 80–81
Strawberry-Almond Overnight Oats, 27
Tropical Fruit Salad, 79
Tropical Smoothie Bowl, 32
Turkey Chili, 147–148
Veggie Omelet, 20

## No heat necessary

Blueberry-Banana Smoothie Bowl, 31–32
Blueberry Overnight Oats, 27
Chocolate and Pretzel Trail Mix, 48
Chocolate, Peanut Butter, and
    Banana Smoothie Bowl, 32
Choose Your Own Frozen Fruit
    Adventure Overnight Oats, 27
Classic Guacamole, 38–39
Fruit Salad with Honey-Citrus
    Dressing, 78–79

Fruit Salad with Mint Dressing, 79
Green Goddess Chopped Salad, 74–75
Matcha-Pineapple Smoothie, 33
Mediterranean Chickpea Salad, 82–83
Melon Salad, 79
No-Bake Butterfinger Pie, 166
No-Bake Candy Bar Pie, 165–166
No-Bake Oreo Pie, 166
No-Bake Twix Pie, 166
Peanut Butter Overnight Oats, 27
Poke Bowl, 145–146
Snickerdoodle Overnight Oats, 26–27
Strawberry-Almond Overnight Oats, 27
Sweet and Salty Trail Mix, 48
Tropical Fruit Salad, 79
Tropical Smoothie Bowl, 32
Tropical Trail Mix, 48

## No nuts

Apple-Cinnamon Baked Oatmeal, 24–25
Apple-Cinnamon Mug Cake, 164
Bacon and Cheese Tater Tot
    Kebabs, 42–43
Bacon-Ranch Chicken, 120–121
Baked Creamy Spinach Ravioli, 91–92
Baked Garlic Butter Cod, 138–139
Baked Vanilla French Toast, 12–13
BBQ Cheeseburger Macaroni, 127
Beef and Broccoli Stir-Fry, 128–129
Blueberry Pancakes, 15
Broccoli-Cheddar Soup, 104–105
Brownie Pie, 167–168
Buffalo Cauliflower Bites, 56–57
Buffalo Chicken Mac and Cheese, 85
California Burger, 113
Cauliflower Parmesan, 99–100
Cheeseburger Macaroni, 126–127
Cheesy Microwave Scramble, 16–17
Cheesy Potato Soup, 106–107
Chicken and Veggie Stir-Fry, 94
Chicken Cheesesteak Quesadilla, 125
Chicken Enchilada Street Fries, 116–117
Chicken Scampi, 137
Chocolate Chip Cookie Bars, 169–170
Cinnamon-Sugar Potato Chips, 50

Classic Chocolate Cake with
    Chocolate Frosting, 160–161
Classic Guacamole, 38–39
Classic Mac and Cheese, 84–85
Classic Turkey Club Sandwiches, 61–62
Cowboy Burgers, 112–113
Creamy Chicken Tortellini Soup, 149–150
Creamy Lentil and Tortellini Soup, 150
Creamy Vegetable Tortellini Soup, 150
Crispy Fish Tacos, 141–142
Crispy Mozzarella Cheese Sticks, 44–45
Deconstructed Spicy-Tangy
    Elote Salad, 76–77
Easy Ground Beef Tacos, 110–111
Easy Shrimp Scampi, 135–137
Everything Bagel Avocado Toast,
    22–23
Everything Bagel Potato Chips, 50
Fluffy Chocolate Chip Pancakes, 14–15
Fruit Salad with Honey-Citrus
    Dressing, 78–79
Fruit Salad with Mint Dressing, 79
Garlic and Onion Potato Chips, 50
Glazed Donut Holes, 175–176
Grilled Cheese Hot Dogs, 114–115
Ham and Cheese Pinwheels, 68–69
Hard- and Soft-Boiled Eggs, 21
Honey-Garlic Pork Chops, 133–134
Honey-Glazed Salmon, 143–144
Italian Cheeseburger Macaroni, 127
Italian Sub Pinwheels, 69
Lasagna Soup, 151–152
Loaded Sheet Pan Nachos, 40–41
Loaded Veggie Quesadilla, 125
Matcha-Pineapple Smoothie, 33
Mediterranean Chickpea Salad, 82–83
Melon Salad, 79
Microwave Potato Chips, 49–50
Monkey Bread, 172–173
Oven-Baked Risotto with Peas, 98
Oven-Fried Chicken Tenders with
    Honey-Mustard Sauce, 118–119
Oven-Toasted Ravioli, 46–47
Parmesan-Crusted Chicken, 122–123
Pasta Primavera, 89–90

Pepperoni Pizza Hand Pies, 67
Perfect Omelet, The, 19–20
Perfect Vanilla Cupcakes with Vanilla
    Buttercream Frosting, 158–159
Pineapple Upside-Down Pancakes, 15
Pizza Omelet, 20
Poke Bowl, 145–146
Potato Chip Cookies, 171
Roast Beef Club Sandwich, 62
Scallop Scampi, 137
Shrimp Tacos, 111
S'more Sundae, 157
Soft-Boiled Egg Avocado Toast, 23
Southwest Quinoa Salad, 80–81
Spaghetti Carbonara, 130–131
Spaghetti Marinara, 86–87
Spicy Nacho Dog Grilled Cheese, 115
Steak and Cheese Hand Pies, 65–67
Steak and Cheese Quesadillas, 124–125
Stir-Fry and Noodles, 94
Strawberry Cheesecake
    Grilled Cheese, 34
Strawberry Sundae, 157
Street Corn Avocado Toast, 23
Stuffed Portabella Mushrooms, 101–103
Taco Tartlets, 54–55
Tropical Burgers, 113
Tropical Fruit Salad, 79
Turkey and Cheese Pinwheels, 69
Turkey Chili, 147–148
Turkey Tacos, 111
Vegetarian Miso Ramen, 95–97
Veggie Omelet, 20
Veggie Scampi, 137
Veggie Stir-Fry, 93–94

## No soy

Apple-Cinnamon Baked Oatmeal, 24–25
Apple-Cinnamon Mug Cake, 164
Apple, Walnut, and Cranberry
    Salad, 72–73
Bacon and Cheese Tater Tot
    Kebabs, 42–43
Baked Creamy Spinach Ravioli, 91–92
Baked Garlic Butter Cod, 138–139
Baked Vanilla French Toast, 12–13
Banana-Walnut Breakfast Couscous, 29
BBQ Cheeseburger Macaroni, 127
Blueberry-Banana Smoothie Bowl, 31–32
Blueberry Breakfast Couscous, 29
Blueberry Overnight Oats, 27
Broccoli-Cheddar Soup, 104–105
Brownie Pie, 167–168
Buffalo Chicken Mac and Cheese, 85
California Burger, 113
Cauliflower Parmesan, 99–100
Cheeseburger Macaroni, 126–127
Cheesy Microwave Scramble, 16–17
Cheesy Potato Soup, 106–107
Chicken Cheesesteak Quesadilla, 125
Chicken Scampi, 137
Chocolate Chip Cookie Bars, 169–170
Choose Your Own Frozen Fruit
    Adventure Overnight Oats, 27
Cinnamon-Raisin Breakfast
    Couscous, 28–29
Cinnamon-Sugar Potato Chips, 50
Classic Chocolate Cake with
    Chocolate Frosting, 160–161
Classic Guacamole, 38–39
Classic Mac and Cheese, 84–85
Cowboy Burgers, 112–113
Creamy Chicken Tortellini Soup, 149–150
Creamy Lentil and Tortellini Soup, 150
Creamy Vegetable Tortellini Soup, 150
Crispy Fish Tacos, 141–142
Crispy Mozzarella Cheese Sticks,
    44–45
Easy Ground Beef Tacos, 110–111
Easy Shrimp Scampi, 135–137
Everything Bagel Avocado Toast, 22–23
Everything Bagel Potato Chips, 50
Fruit Salad with Honey-Citrus
    Dressing, 78–79
Fruit Salad with Mint Dressing, 79
Garlic and Onion Potato Chips, 50
Hard- and Soft-Boiled Eggs, 21
Italian Cheeseburger Macaroni, 127
Lasagna Soup, 151–152
Loaded Sheet Pan Nachos, 40–41

Loaded Veggie Quesadilla, 125
Maple Granola with Cranberries, 51–53
Matcha-Pineapple Smoothie, 33
Mediterranean Chickpea Salad, 82–83
Melon Salad, 79
Microwave Potato Chips, 49–50
Oven-Baked Risotto with Peas, 98
Oven-Toasted Ravioli, 46–47
Pasta Primavera, 89–90
Peanut Butter and Banana Panini, 58–59
Peanut Butter Overnight Oats, 27
Perfect Omelet, The, 19–20
Perfect Vanilla Cupcakes with Vanilla
    Buttercream Frosting, 158–159
Pizza Omelet, 20
Potato Chip Cookies, 171
Scallop Scampi, 137
Shrimp Tacos, 111
Snickerdoodle Overnight Oats,
    26–27
Soft-Boiled Egg Avocado Toast, 23
Southwest Quinoa Salad, 80–81
Spaghetti Carbonara, 130–131
Spaghetti Marinara, 86–87
Steak and Cheese Quesadillas, 124–125
Strawberry-Almond Overnight Oats, 27
Strawberry Cheesecake
    Grilled Cheese, 34
Strawberry-Pecan Breakfast
    Couscous, 29
Street Corn Avocado Toast, 23
Stuffed Portabella Mushrooms,
    101–103
Tropical Burgers, 113
Tropical Fruit Salad, 79
Turkey Chili, 147–148
Turkey Tacos, 111
Veggie Omelet, 20
Veggie Scampi, 137

## Really fast (10 minutes or less)

Apple-Cinnamon Mug Cake, 164
Blueberry-Banana Smoothie Bowl, 31–32
Cheesy Microwave Scramble, 16–17
Chocolate and Pretzel Trail Mix, 48

Chocolate, Peanut Butter, and
    Banana Smoothie Bowl, 32
Classic Guacamole, 38–39
Everything Bagel Avocado Toast, 22–23
Fruit Salad with Honey-Citrus
    Dressing, 78–79
Fruit Salad with Mint Dressing, 79
Green Goddess Chopped Salad, 74–75
Matcha-Pineapple Smoothie, 33
Mediterranean Chickpea Salad, 82–83
Melon Salad, 79
Peanut Butter and Banana Panini, 58–59
S'more Sundae, 157
Strawberry Sundae, 157
Sweet and Salty Trail Mix, 48
Tropical Fruit Salad, 79
Tropical Smoothie Bowl, 32
Tropical Trail Mix, 48

## Vegan

Blueberry Overnight Oats, 27
Choose Your Own Frozen Fruit
    Adventure Overnight Oats, 27
Cinnamon-Sugar Potato Chips, 50
Classic Guacamole, 38–39
Everything Bagel Avocado Toast, 22–23
Everything Bagel Potato Chips, 50
Garlic and Onion Potato Chips, 50
Maple Granola with Cranberries, 51–53
Mediterranean Chickpea Salad, 82–83
Microwave Potato Chips, 49–50
Peanut Butter Overnight Oats, 27
Snickerdoodle Overnight Oats, 26–27
Strawberry-Almond Overnight Oats, 27

## Vegetarian

Apple-Cinnamon Baked Oatmeal, 24–25
Apple-Cinnamon Mug Cake, 164
Apple, Walnut, and Cranberry
    Salad, 72–73
Baked Creamy Spinach Ravioli, 91–92
Baked Vanilla French Toast, 12–13
Banana-Walnut Breakfast Couscous, 29
Banana-Walnut Pancakes, 15
Blueberry-Banana Smoothie Bowl, 31–32

Blueberry Breakfast Couscous, 29
Blueberry Pancakes, 15
Broccoli-Cheddar Soup, 104–105
Brownie Pie, 167–168
Buffalo Cauliflower Bites, 56–57
Cauliflower Parmesan, 99–100
Cheesy Microwave Scramble, 16–17
Chocolate and Pretzel Trail Mix, 48
Chocolate Chip Cookie Bars, 169–170
Chocolate, Peanut Butter, and
    Banana Smoothie Bowl, 32
Cinnamon-Raisin Breakfast
    Couscous, 28–29
Classic Chocolate Cake with
    Chocolate Frosting, 160–161
Classic Mac and Cheese, 84–85
Crispy Mozzarella Cheese Sticks, 44–45
Deconstructed Spicy-Tangy
    Elote Salad, 76–77
Fluffy Chocolate Chip Pancakes, 14–15
Fruit Salad with Honey-Citrus
    Dressing, 78–79
Fruit Salad with Mint Dressing, 79
Glazed Donut Holes, 175–176
Green Goddess Chopped Salad, 74–75
Hard- and Soft-Boiled Eggs, 21
Matcha-Pineapple Smoothie, 33
Melon Salad, 79
Monkey Bread, 172–173
No-Bake Butterfinger Pie, 166

No-Bake Candy Bar Pie, 165–166
No-Bake Oreo Pie, 166
No-Bake Twix Pie, 166
Oven-Toasted Ravioli, 46–47
Pasta Primavera, 89–90
Peanut Butter and Banana Panini, 58–59
Perfect Omelet, The, 19–20
Perfect Vanilla Cupcakes with Vanilla
    Buttercream Frosting, 158–159
Pineapple Upside-Down Pancakes, 15
Potato Chip Cookies, 171
Snickerdoodle Poke Cake, 162–163
Soft-Boiled Egg Avocado Toast, 23
Southwest Quinoa Salad, 80–81
Spaghetti Marinara, 86–87
Stir-Fry and Noodles, 94
Strawberry Cheesecake
    Grilled Cheese, 34
Strawberry-Pecan Breakfast
    Couscous, 29
Street Corn Avocado Toast, 23
Stuffed Portabella Mushrooms, 101–103
Sweet and Salty Trail Mix, 48
Tropical Fruit Salad, 79
Tropical Smoothie Bowl, 32
Tropical Trail Mix, 48
Vegetarian Miso Ramen, 95–97
Veggie Omelet, 20
Veggie Stir-Fry, 93–94

# Index

## A

Appetizers. *See* Snacks and appetizers

Apples
 Apple-Cinnamon Baked
  Oatmeal, 24–25
 Apple-Cinnamon Mug Cake, 164
 Apple, Walnut, and Cranberry
  Salad, 72–73
 Fruit Salad with Honey-Citrus
  Dressing, 78–79
 Fruit Salad with Mint Dressing, 79

Arugula
 Green Goddess Chopped Salad, 74–75

Avocados
 California Burger, 113
 Classic Guacamole, 38–39
 Everything Bagel Avocado Toast, 22–23
 Green Goddess Chopped Salad, 74–75
 Soft-Boiled Egg Avocado Toast, 23
 Southwest Quinoa Salad, 80–81
 Street Corn Avocado Toast, 23

## B

Bacon
 Bacon and Cheese Tater
  Tot Kebabs, 42–43
 Bacon-Ranch Chicken, 120–121
 Cheesy Potato Soup, 106–107
 Classic Turkey Club Sandwiches,
  61–62
 Roast Beef Club Sandwich, 62
 Spaghetti Carbonara, 130–131

Baked Creamy Spinach Ravioli, 91–92
Baked Garlic Butter Cod, 138–139
Baked Vanilla French Toast, 12–13
Bakeware, 4

Bananas
 Banana-Walnut Breakfast Couscous, 29
 Banana-Walnut Pancakes, 15
 Blueberry-Banana Smoothie
  Bowl, 31–32
 Chocolate and Pretzel Trail Mix, 48
 Chocolate, Peanut Butter, and
  Banana Smoothie Bowl, 32
 Fruit Salad with Honey-Citrus
  Dressing, 78–79
 Fruit Salad with Mint Dressing, 79
 Peanut Butter and Banana
  Panini, 58–59
 Sweet and Salty Trail Mix, 48
 Tropical Fruit Salad, 79
 Tropical Smoothie Bowl, 32
 Tropical Trail Mix, 48

Basil
 Cauliflower Parmesan, 99–100
 Green Goddess Chopped Salad, 74–75

BBQ Cheeseburger Macaroni, 127

Beans
 Chicken Enchilada Street Fries, 116–117
 Loaded Sheet Pan Nachos, 40–41

Southwest Quinoa Salad, 80–81
Turkey Chili, 147–148
Beef
  BBQ Cheeseburger Macaroni, 127
  Beef and Broccoli Stir-Fry, 128–129
  California Burger, 113
  Cheeseburger Macaroni, 126–127
  Cowboy Burgers, 112–113
  Easy Ground Beef Tacos, 110–111
  Italian Cheeseburger Macaroni, 127
  Lasagna Soup, 151–152
  Loaded Sheet Pan Nachos, 40–41
  Roast Beef Club Sandwich, 62
  Steak and Cheese Hand Pies, 65–67
  Steak and Cheese Quesadillas, 124–125
  Taco Tartlets, 54–55
  Tropical Burgers, 113
Berries
  Apple, Walnut, and Cranberry
    Salad, 72–73
  Blueberry-Banana Smoothie
    Bowl, 31–32
  Blueberry Breakfast Couscous, 29
  Blueberry Overnight Oats, 27
  Blueberry Pancakes, 15
  Fruit Salad with Honey-Citrus
    Dressing, 78–79
  Fruit Salad with Mint Dressing, 79
  Maple Granola with Cranberries, 51–53
  Melon Salad, 79
  Strawberry-Almond Overnight Oats, 27
  Strawberry Cheesecake
    Grilled Cheese, 34
  Strawberry-Pecan Breakfast
    Couscous, 29
  Strawberry Sundae, 157
  Sweet and Salty Trail Mix, 48
  Tropical Fruit Salad, 79
  Turkey and Cheese Pinwheels, 69
Biscuit dough
  Glazed Donut Holes, 175–176
  Monkey Bread, 172–173
Blueberry-Banana Smoothie Bowl, 31–32
Blueberry Breakfast Couscous, 29
Blueberry Overnight Oats, 27

Blueberry Pancakes, 15
Boiling, 178
Bowls
  Blueberry-Banana Smoothie
    Bowl, 31–32
  Chocolate, Peanut Butter, and
    Banana Smoothie Bowl, 32
  Poke Bowl, 145–146
  Tropical Smoothie Bowl, 32
Bread
  Baked Vanilla French Toast, 12–13
  Classic Turkey Club Sandwiches, 61–62
  Everything Bagel Avocado Toast, 22–23
  Grilled Cheese Hot Dogs, 114–115
  Peanut Butter and Banana
    Panini, 58–59
  Roast Beef Club Sandwich, 62
  Soft-Boiled Egg Avocado Toast, 23
  Spicy Nacho Dog Grilled Cheese, 115
  Strawberry Cheesecake
    Grilled Cheese, 34
  Street Corn Avocado Toast, 23
Broccoli
  Beef and Broccoli Stir-Fry, 128–129
  Broccoli-Cheddar Soup, 104–105
  Creamy Vegetable Tortellini Soup, 150
  Veggie Omelet, 20
Brownie Pie, 167–168
Buffalo Cauliflower Bites, 56–57
Buffalo Chicken Mac and Cheese, 85
Burgers
  California Burger, 113
  Cowboy Burgers, 112–113
  Tropical Burgers, 113
Burn safety, 6

C
California Burger, 113
Candy
  No-Bake Butterfinger Pie, 166
  No-Bake Candy Bar Pie, 165–166
  No-Bake Twix Pie, 166
Canola oil, 9
Cantaloupe
  Melon Salad, 79

Capocollo
  Italian Sub Pinwheels, 69
Caramel
  No-Bake Candy Bar Pie, 165–166
  No-Bake Twix Pie, 166
Carrots
  Broccoli-Cheddar Soup, 104–105
  Chicken and Veggie Stir-Fry, 94
  Creamy Chicken Tortellini
    Soup, 149–150
  Creamy Lentil and Tortellini Soup, 150
  Creamy Vegetable Tortellini Soup, 150
  Poke Bowl, 145–146
  Stir-Fry and Noodles, 94
  Veggie Stir-Fry, 93–94
Cauliflower
  Buffalo Cauliflower Bites, 56–57
  Cauliflower Parmesan, 99–100
  Creamy Vegetable Tortellini Soup, 150
Celery
  Creamy Chicken Tortellini
    Soup, 149–150
  Creamy Lentil and Tortellini Soup, 150
  Creamy Vegetable Tortellini Soup, 150
  Roasted Chicken Salad Pitas, 63–64
Cheese. See also Cream cheese
  Apple, Walnut, and Cranberry
    Salad, 72–73
  Bacon and Cheese Tater
    Tot Kebabs, 42–43
  Bacon-Ranch Chicken, 120–121
  Baked Creamy Spinach Ravioli, 91–92
  BBQ Cheeseburger Macaroni, 127
  Broccoli-Cheddar Soup, 104–105
  Buffalo Chicken Mac and Cheese, 85
  California Burger, 113
  Cauliflower Parmesan, 99–100
  Cheeseburger Macaroni, 126–127
  Cheesy Microwave Scramble, 16–17
  Chicken Cheesesteak Quesadilla, 125
  Chicken Enchilada Street Fries, 116–117
  Classic Mac and Cheese, 84–85
  Cowboy Burgers, 112–113
  Crispy Mozzarella Cheese Sticks,
    44–45

  Deconstructed Spicy-Tangy
    Elote Salad, 76–77
  Green Goddess Chopped Salad, 74–75
  Grilled Cheese Hot Dogs, 114–115
  Ham and Cheese Pinwheels, 68–69
  Italian Cheeseburger Macaroni, 127
  Italian Sub Pinwheels, 69
  Lasagna Soup, 151–152
  Loaded Sheet Pan Nachos, 40–41
  Loaded Veggie Quesadilla, 125
  Oven-Baked Risotto with Peas, 98
  Oven-Toasted Ravioli, 46–47
  Parmesan-Crusted Chicken, 122–123
  Pasta Primavera, 89–90
  Pepperoni Pizza Hand Pies, 67
  Pizza Omelet, 20
  Roasted Chicken Salad Pitas, 63–64
  Spaghetti Carbonara, 130–131
  Spaghetti Marinara, 86–87
  Spicy Nacho Dog Grilled Cheese, 115
  Steak and Cheese Hand Pies, 65–67
  Steak and Cheese Quesadillas, 124–125
  Street Corn Avocado Toast, 23
  Stuffed Portabella Mushrooms, 101–103
  Taco Tartlets, 54–55
  Tropical Burgers, 113
  Turkey and Cheese Pinwheels, 69
Cheeseburger Macaroni, 126–127
Cheesy Microwave Scramble, 16–17
Cheesy Potato Soup, 106–107
Cherries
  Pineapple Upside-Down Pancakes, 15
  Strawberry Sundae, 157
Chia seeds
  Blueberry-Banana Smoothie Bowl, 31–32
  Snickerdoodle Overnight Oats, 26–27
  Tropical Smoothie Bowl, 32
Chicken
  Bacon-Ranch Chicken, 120–121
  Buffalo Chicken Mac and Cheese, 85
  canned, 9
  Chicken and Veggie Stir-Fry, 94
  Chicken Cheesesteak Quesadilla, 125
  Chicken Enchilada Street Fries, 116–117
  Chicken Scampi, 137

Creamy Chicken Tortellini
    Soup, 149–150
Oven-Fried Chicken Tenders with
    Honey-Mustard Sauce, 118–119
Parmesan-Crusted Chicken, 122–123
Roasted Chicken Salad Pitas, 63–64
Chickpea Salad, Mediterranean, 82–83
Chocolate
    Brownie Pie, 167–168
    Chocolate and Pretzel Trail Mix, 48
    Chocolate Chip Cookie Bars, 169–170
    Chocolate, Peanut Butter, and
        Banana Smoothie Bowl, 32
    Classic Chocolate Cake with
        Chocolate Frosting, 160–161
    Fluffy Chocolate Chip Pancakes, 14–15
    No-Bake Candy Bar Pie, 165–166
    S'more Sundae, 157
    Sweet and Salty Trail Mix, 48
Choose Your Own Frozen Fruit
    Adventure Overnight Oats, 27
Chopping, 178
Cilantro
    Classic Guacamole, 38–39
    Deconstructed Spicy-Tangy
        Elote Salad, 76–77
    Southwest Quinoa Salad, 80–81
    Street Corn Avocado Toast, 23
Cinnamon-Raisin Breakfast
        Couscous, 28–29
Cinnamon-Sugar Potato Chips, 50
Classic Chocolate Cake with
    Chocolate Frosting, 160–161
Classic Guacamole, 38–39
Classic Mac and Cheese, 84–85
Classic Turkey Club Sandwiches, 61–62
Cleaning up, 3
Coconut
    Maple Granola with Cranberries, 51–53
    Tropical Smoothie Bowl, 32
Cod
    Baked Garlic Butter Cod, 138–139
    Crispy Fish Tacos, 141–142
Coleslaw
    Crispy Fish Tacos, 141–142

Consistency, 178
Cookware, 4
Corn
    Chicken Enchilada Street Fries, 116–117
    Deconstructed Spicy-Tangy
        Elote Salad, 76–77
    Loaded Sheet Pan Nachos, 40–41
    Southwest Quinoa Salad, 80–81
    Street Corn Avocado Toast, 23
Couscous
    Banana-Walnut Breakfast Couscous, 29
    Blueberry Breakfast Couscous, 29
    Cinnamon-Raisin Breakfast
        Couscous, 28–29
    Strawberry-Pecan Breakfast
        Couscous, 29
Cowboy Burgers, 112–113
Crackers
    Sweet and Salty Trail Mix, 48
Cream cheese
    No-Bake Butterfinger Pie, 166
    No-Bake Oreo Pie, 166
    Steak and Cheese Hand Pies, 65–67
    Strawberry Cheesecake
        Grilled Cheese, 34
    Stuffed Portabella Mushrooms, 101–103
Creamy Chicken Tortellini Soup, 149–150
Creamy Lentil and Tortellini Soup, 150
Creamy Vegetable Tortellini Soup, 150
Crescent rolls
    Pepperoni Pizza Hand Pies, 67
    Steak and Cheese Hand Pies, 65–67
Crispy Fish Tacos, 141–142
Crispy Mozzarella Cheese Sticks,
    44–45
Cross-contamination, 2–3, 7
Crosswise slicing, 178
Cucumbers
    Mediterranean Chickpea Salad, 82–83
    Poke Bowl, 145–146

## D

Dash, 178
Deconstructed Spicy-Tangy
        Elote Salad, 76–77

Desserts
  Apple-Cinnamon Mug Cake, 164
  Brownie Pie, 167–168
  Chocolate Chip Cookie Bars, 169–170
  Classic Chocolate Cake with
    Chocolate Frosting, 160–161
  Glazed Donut Holes, 175–176
  Monkey Bread, 172–173
  No-Bake Butterfinger Pie, 166
  No-Bake Candy Bar Pie, 165–166
  No-Bake Oreo Pie, 166
  No-Bake Twix Pie, 166
  Orange Dream Poke Cake, 163
  Perfect Vanilla Cupcakes with
    Vanilla Buttercream
    Frosting, 158–159
  Potato Chip Cookies, 171
  S'more Sundae, 157
  Snickerdoodle Poke Cake,
    162–163
  Strawberry Poke Cake, 163
  Strawberry Sundae, 157
Dicing, 178
Dividing, 178
Dredging, 178

### E

Easy Ground Beef Tacos, 110–111
Easy Shrimp Scampi, 135–137
Edamame
  Poke Bowl, 145–146
Eggs
  Baked Vanilla French Toast, 12–13
  Cheesy Microwave Scramble, 16–17
  Hard- and Soft-Boiled Eggs, 21
  Perfect Omelet, The, 19–20
  Pizza Omelet, 20
  Soft-Boiled Egg Avocado Toast, 23
  Spaghetti Carbonara, 130–131
  Vegetarian Miso Ramen, 95–97
  Veggie Omelet, 20
Equipment, 4
Everything Bagel Avocado Toast,
  22–23
Everything Bagel Potato Chips, 50

### F

Fish
  Baked Garlic Butter Cod, 138–139
  Crispy Fish Tacos, 141–142
  Honey-Glazed Salmon, 143–144
  Poke Bowl, 145–146
Flaxseed
  Maple Granola with Cranberries, 51–53
  Matcha-Pineapple Smoothie, 33
Flour, 9
Fluffy Chocolate Chip Pancakes, 14–15
Food safety, 2–3
Fruits. *See also specific*
  Choose Your Own Frozen Fruit
    Adventure Overnight Oats, 27
Fruit Salad with Honey-Citrus
  Dressing, 78–79
Fruit Salad with Mint Dressing, 79

### G

Garbage bowls, 3
Garlic, 9
Garlic and Onion Potato Chips, 50
Ginger
  Beef and Broccoli Stir-Fry, 128–129
  Chicken and Veggie Stir-Fry, 94
  Stir-Fry and Noodles, 94
  Vegetarian Miso Ramen, 95–97
  Veggie Stir-Fry, 93–94
Glazed Donut Holes, 175–176
Graham crackers
  No-Bake Candy Bar Pie, 165–166
  No-Bake Twix Pie, 166
  S'more Sundae, 157
Grapes
  Fruit Salad with Honey-Citrus
    Dressing, 78–79
  Fruit Salad with Mint Dressing, 79
Green beans
  Chicken and Veggie Stir-Fry, 94
  Stir-Fry and Noodles, 94
  Veggie Stir-Fry, 93–94
Green Goddess Chopped Salad, 74–75
Greens. *See also specific*

Apple, Walnut, and Cranberry
 Salad, 72–73
Grilled Cheese Hot Dogs, 114–115

## H

Ham and Cheese Pinwheels, 68–69
Handwashing, 3, 7
Hard- and Soft-Boiled Eggs, 21
Honeydew
 Melon Salad, 79
Honey-Garlic Pork Chops, 133–134
Honey-Glazed Salmon, 143–144
Hot dogs
 Grilled Cheese Hot Dogs, 114–115
 Spicy Nacho Dog Grilled Cheese, 115

## I

Ice cream
 S'more Sundae, 157
 Strawberry Sundae, 157
Italian Cheeseburger Macaroni, 127
Italian Sub Pinwheels, 69

## K

Kitchen prep, 2–3
Kiwis
 Fruit Salad with Honey-Citrus
  Dressing, 78–79
 Fruit Salad with Mint Dressing, 79
 Melon Salad, 79
 Tropical Fruit Salad, 79
Knife safety, 6

## L

Lasagna Soup, 151–152
Lengthwise slicing, 178
Lentil and Tortellini Soup,
 Creamy, 150
Lettuce
 California Burger, 113
 Classic Turkey Club Sandwiches,
  61–62
 Roast Beef Club Sandwich, 62
Loaded Sheet Pan Nachos, 40–41
Loaded Veggie Quesadilla, 125

## M

Mangos
 Tropical Fruit Salad, 79
 Tropical Smoothie Bowl, 32
Maple Granola with Cranberries, 51–53
Maple syrup
 Maple Granola with Cranberries, 51–53
 Peanut Butter Overnight Oats, 27
Marshmallows
 S'more Sundae, 157
Mashing, 178
Matcha-Pineapple Smoothie, 33
Measuring, 3
Mediterranean Chickpea Salad, 82–83
Melon Salad, 79
Microwave Potato Chips, 49–50
Microwaves, 5
Mincing, 178
Mint Dressing, Fruit Salad with, 79
Miso Ramen, Vegetarian, 95–97
Monkey Bread, 172–173
Mushrooms
 Chicken and Veggie Stir-Fry, 94
 Loaded Veggie Quesadilla, 125
 Stir-Fry and Noodles, 94
 Stuffed Portabella Mushrooms, 101–103
 Vegetarian Miso Ramen, 95–97
 Veggie Omelet, 20
 Veggie Stir-Fry, 93–94

## N

No-Bake Butterfinger Pie, 166
No-Bake Candy Bar Pie, 165–166
No-Bake Oreo Pie, 166
No-Bake Twix Pie, 166
Noodles
 Stir-Fry and Noodles, 94
 Vegetarian Miso Ramen, 95–97
Nut butters, 9
Nuts
 Apple, Walnut, and Cranberry
  Salad, 72–73
 Banana-Walnut Breakfast Couscous, 29
 Banana-Walnut Pancakes, 15

Nuts (*continued*)
Blueberry Breakfast Couscous, 29
Chocolate and Pretzel Trail Mix, 48
Chocolate, Peanut Butter, and
Banana Smoothie Bowl, 32
Cinnamon-Raisin Breakfast
Couscous, 28–29
Maple Granola with Cranberries, 51–53
No-Bake Candy Bar Pie, 165–166
Roasted Chicken Salad Pitas, 63–64
Strawberry-Almond Overnight Oats, 27
Strawberry-Pecan Breakfast
Couscous, 29
Sweet and Salty Trail Mix, 48
Tropical Trail Mix, 48

## O

Oats
Apple-Cinnamon Baked
Oatmeal, 24–25
Blueberry Overnight Oats, 27
Choose Your Own Frozen Fruit
Adventure Overnight Oats, 27
Maple Granola with Cranberries, 51–53
Peanut Butter Overnight Oats, 27
Snickerdoodle Overnight Oats, 26–27
Strawberry-Almond Overnight Oats, 27
Olive oil, 9
Orange Dream Poke Cake, 163
Oranges
Fruit Salad with Honey-Citrus
Dressing, 78–79
Fruit Salad with Mint Dressing, 79
Melon Salad, 79
Tropical Fruit Salad, 79
Tropical Smoothie Bowl, 32
Oven-Baked Risotto with Peas, 98
Oven-Fried Chicken Tenders with
Honey-Mustard Sauce, 118–119
Oven-Toasted Ravioli, 46–47

## P

Pantry staples, 8–9
Parmesan-Crusted Chicken, 122–123
Parsley

Chicken Scampi, 137
Easy Shrimp Scampi, 135–137
Mediterranean Chickpea Salad, 82–83
Scallop Scampi, 137
Veggie Scampi, 137
Pasta, 8
Baked Creamy Spinach Ravioli, 91–92
BBQ Cheeseburger Macaroni, 127
Buffalo Chicken Mac and Cheese, 85
Cheeseburger Macaroni, 126–127
Chicken Scampi, 137
Classic Mac and Cheese, 84–85
Creamy Chicken Tortellini
Soup, 149–150
Creamy Lentil and Tortellini Soup, 150
Creamy Vegetable Tortellini Soup, 150
Easy Shrimp Scampi, 135–137
Italian Cheeseburger Macaroni, 127
Lasagna Soup, 151–152
Oven-Toasted Ravioli, 46–47
Pasta Primavera, 89–90
Scallop Scampi, 137
Spaghetti Carbonara, 130–131
Spaghetti Marinara, 86–87
Veggie Scampi, 137
Pasta Primavera, 89–90
Peanut butter
Chocolate, Peanut Butter, and
Banana Smoothie Bowl, 32
Peanut Butter and Banana
Panini, 58–59
Peanut Butter Overnight Oats, 27
Peas, Oven-Baked Risotto with, 98
Pepperoni
Italian Sub Pinwheels, 69
Pepperoni Pizza Hand Pies, 67
Pizza Omelet, 20
Peppers
Chicken Cheesesteak Quesadilla, 125
Classic Guacamole, 38–39
Loaded Sheet Pan Nachos, 40–41
Loaded Veggie Quesadilla, 125
Mediterranean Chickpea Salad, 82–83
Southwest Quinoa Salad, 80–81
Steak and Cheese Quesadillas, 124–125

Stuffed Portabella Mushrooms, 101–103

Turkey Chili, 147–148

Veggie Omelet, 20

Perfect Omelet, The, 19–20

Perfect Vanilla Cupcakes with Vanilla
    Buttercream Frosting, 158–159

Phyllo shells

Taco Tartlets, 54–55

Pinch, 178

Pineapple

Matcha-Pineapple Smoothie, 33

Pineapple Upside-Down Pancakes, 15

Tropical Burgers, 113

Tropical Fruit Salad, 79

Tropical Smoothie Bowl, 32

Tropical Trail Mix, 48

Pineapple Upside-Down Pancakes, 15

Pizza dough

Ham and Cheese Pinwheels, 68–69

Italian Sub Pinwheels, 69

Turkey and Cheese Pinwheels, 69

Pizza Omelet, 20

Poke Bowl, 145–146

Pork Chops, Honey-Garlic, 133–134

Potato chips

Cinnamon-Sugar Potato Chips, 50

Everything Bagel Potato Chips, 50

Garlic and Onion Potato Chips, 50

Microwave Potato Chips, 49–50

Potato Chip Cookies, 171

Roasted Chicken Salad Pitas, 63–64

Potatoes

Bacon and Cheese Tater
    Tot Kebabs, 42–43

Cheesy Potato Soup, 106–107

Chicken Enchilada Street Fries, 116–117

Cinnamon-Sugar Potato Chips, 50

Everything Bagel Potato Chips, 50

Garlic and Onion Potato Chips, 50

Microwave Potato Chips, 49–50

Preheating, 178

Pretzel and Chocolate Trail Mix, 48

Produce washing, 2

Prosciutto

Italian Sub Pinwheels, 69

Q

Quinoa Salad, Southwest, 80–81

R

Raisins

Cinnamon-Raisin Breakfast
    Couscous, 28–29

Tropical Trail Mix, 48

Recipes, about, 2

Resting, 179

Rice, 8

Oven-Baked Risotto with Peas, 98

Poke Bowl, 145–146

Roast Beef Club Sandwich, 62

Roasted Chicken Salad Pitas, 63–64

Room temperature, 179

S

Safety

burns, 6

food, 2–3, 7

knives, 6

Salads

Apple, Walnut, and Cranberry
    Salad, 72–73

Deconstructed Spicy-Tangy
    Elote Salad, 76–77

Fruit Salad with Honey-Citrus
    Dressing, 78–79

Fruit Salad with Mint Dressing, 79

Green Goddess Chopped Salad, 74–75

Mediterranean Chickpea Salad, 82–83

Southwest Quinoa Salad, 80–81

Tropical Fruit Salad, 79

Salami

Italian Sub Pinwheels, 69

Salmon, Honey-Glazed, 143–144

Sandwiches. *See also* Burgers

Classic Turkey Club Sandwiches,
    61–62

Everything Bagel Avocado Toast, 22–23

Grilled Cheese Hot Dogs, 114–115

Ham and Cheese Pinwheels, 68–69

Italian Sub Pinwheels, 69

Sandwiches (*continued*)
  Peanut Butter and Banana
      Panini, 58–59
  Pepperoni Pizza Hand Pies, 67
  Roast Beef Club Sandwich, 62
  Roasted Chicken Salad Pitas, 63–64
  Soft-Boiled Egg Avocado Toast, 23
  Spicy Nacho Dog Grilled Cheese, 115
  Steak and Cheese Hand Pies, 65–67
  Strawberry Cheesecake
      Grilled Cheese, 34
  Street Corn Avocado Toast, 23
  Turkey and Cheese Pinwheels, 69
Scallop Scampi, 137
Seasonings, 8
Serrated blades, 179
Shredding, 179
Shrimp
  Easy Shrimp Scampi, 135–137
  Shrimp Tacos, 111
Simmering, 179
Smoothies
  Blueberry-Banana Smoothie
      Bowl, 31–32
  Chocolate, Peanut Butter, and
      Banana Smoothie Bowl, 32
  Matcha-Pineapple Smoothie, 33
  Tropical Smoothie Bowl, 32
S'more Sundae, 157
Snacks and appetizers
  Bacon and Cheese Tater
      Tot Kebabs, 42–43
  Buffalo Cauliflower Bites, 56–57
  Chocolate and Pretzel Trail Mix, 48
  Cinnamon-Sugar Potato Chips, 50
  Classic Guacamole, 38–39
  Crispy Mozzarella Cheese Sticks, 44–45
  Everything Bagel Potato Chips, 50
  Garlic and Onion Potato Chips, 50
  Loaded Sheet Pan Nachos, 40–41
  Maple Granola with Cranberries, 51–53
  Microwave Potato Chips, 49–50
  Oven-Toasted Ravioli, 46–47
  Sweet and Salty Trail Mix, 48
  Taco Tartlets, 54–55

  Tropical Trail Mix, 48
Snickerdoodle Overnight Oats, 26–27
Snickerdoodle Poke Cake, 162–163
Soft-Boiled Egg Avocado Toast, 23
Soups
  Broccoli-Cheddar Soup, 104–105
  Cheesy Potato Soup, 106–107
  Creamy Chicken Tortellini
      Soup, 149–150
  Creamy Lentil and Tortellini Soup, 150
  Creamy Vegetable Tortellini Soup, 150
  Lasagna Soup, 151–152
  Turkey Chili, 147–148
  Vegetarian Miso Ramen, 95–97
Sour cream
  Cheesy Potato Soup, 106–107
  Chicken Enchilada Street Fries, 116–117
  Southwest Quinoa Salad, 80–81
Soy sauce, 9
Spaghetti Carbonara, 130–131
Spaghetti Marinara, 86–87
Spicy Nacho Dog Grilled Cheese, 115
Spinach
  Baked Creamy Spinach Ravioli, 91–92
  Creamy Chicken Tortellini
      Soup, 149–150
  Creamy Lentil and Tortellini Soup, 150
  Creamy Vegetable Tortellini Soup, 150
  Green Goddess Chopped Salad, 74–75
  Loaded Veggie Quesadilla, 125
  Matcha-Pineapple Smoothie, 33
  Stuffed Portabella Mushrooms, 101–103
  Vegetarian Miso Ramen, 95–97
Standing, 179
Starches, 8
Steak and Cheese Hand Pies, 65–67
Steak and Cheese Quesadillas, 124–125
Stir-Fry and Noodles, 94
Stocks, 8
Strawberry-Almond Overnight Oats, 27
Strawberry Cheesecake
    Grilled Cheese, 34
Strawberry-Pecan Breakfast
    Couscous, 29
Strawberry Poke Cake, 163

Strawberry Sundae, 157
Street Corn Avocado Toast, 23
Stuffed Portabella Mushrooms, 101–103
Substituting, 179
Sweet and Salty Trail Mix, 48

## T

Tacos
  Crispy Fish Tacos, 141–142
  Easy Ground Beef Tacos, 110–111
  Shrimp Tacos, 111
  Turkey Tacos, 111
Taco Tartlets, 54–55
Tomatoes
  California Burger, 113
  Classic Guacamole, 38–39
  Classic Turkey Club Sandwiches, 61–62
  Loaded Sheet Pan Nachos, 40–41
  Loaded Veggie Quesadilla, 125
  Roast Beef Club Sandwich, 62
  Spaghetti Marinara, 86–87
  Stuffed Portabella Mushrooms, 101–103
  Turkey Chili, 147–148
  Veggie Omelet, 20
  Veggie Scampi, 137
Tools, 4
Tortilla chips
  Loaded Sheet Pan Nachos, 40–41
Tortillas
  Chicken Cheesesteak Quesadilla, 125
  Crispy Fish Tacos, 141–142
  Easy Ground Beef Tacos, 110–111
  Loaded Veggie Quesadilla, 125
  Shrimp Tacos, 111
  Steak and Cheese Quesadillas, 124–125
  Turkey Tacos, 111
Transferring, 179
Tropical Burger, 113
Tropical Fruit Salad, 79
Tropical Smoothie Bowl, 32
Tropical Trail Mix, 48
Tuna
  canned, 9
  Poke Bowl, 145–146
Turkey

Classic Turkey Club Sandwiches, 61–62
Turkey and Cheese Pinwheels, 69
Turkey Chili, 147–148
Turkey Tacos, 111

## U
Utensils, 4

## V
Vanilla extract, 9
Vegetables. *See also specific*
  Pasta Primavera, 89–90
Vegetarian Miso Ramen, 95–97
Veggie Omelet, 20
Veggie Scampi, 137
Veggie Stir-Fry, 93–94

## W
Watermelon
  Melon Salad, 79
Whipped topping
  No-Bake Butterfinger Pie, 166
  No-Bake Candy Bar Pie, 165–166
  No-Bake Oreo Pie, 166
  No-Bake Twix Pie, 166
  Snickerdoodle Poke Cake, 162–163
  Strawberry Sundae, 157
Whisking, 179

## Y
Yogurt
  Blueberry-Banana Smoothie
    Bowl, 31–32
  Chocolate, Peanut Butter, and
    Banana Smoothie Bowl, 32
  Green Goddess Chopped Salad, 74–75
  Matcha-Pineapple Smoothie, 33
  Tropical Smoothie Bowl, 32

## Z
Zucchini
  Veggie Scampi, 137

# Acknowledgments

To Joey, my faithful sous chef and trusted taste tester. Our time in the kitchen means the world to me. There is nothing I love more than making these memories with you. You are the inspiration for this book.

To Jim, my constant support system who's always there when I need you. Thank you for always supporting me and encouraging me to follow my dreams. Without your nudge, I wouldn't have embarked on this crazy ride.

To my mom and dad, you always were my biggest cheerleaders. I appreciate all you've done for me, more than you know.

To my grandmothers, thank you for your patience and love and for inspiring my love of cooking. I treasure the memories I have of cooking alongside each of you.

To my mother-in-law, your recipes are legendary and I cherish the times we've spent cooking together.

To the rest of my family and friends, thank you for your continued support. You all inspire me every day.

To the Callisto team, thank you for bringing this book to life. I hope it inspires those who read it to create amazing recipes and spend time in the kitchen.

# About the Author

Christina Hitchcock is the creator and owner of the popular food blog It Is a Keeper (ItIsaKeeper.com). Her passion is sharing quick and easy recipes for busy families using easy-to-find, everyday ingredients. Christina discovered her love for cooking by spending time with her grandmothers in the kitchen. Her award-winning recipes have been featured on television, in national magazines, and on numerous online sites. Christina lives in northeast Pennsylvania with her husband and son. Follow her on Facebook (@itsakeeper), Instagram, YouTube, Twitter, and Pinterest (@itsakeeperblog).